The Voice of Faith

A Teen Study of

Psalms

Andrew Phillips & James Hayes

ISBN: 978-0-89098-901-2

©2015 by 21st Century Christian

2809 12th Ave S, Nashville, TN 37204

All rights reserved.

Cover design by Jonathan Edelhuber

Table of Content

James wrote chapters 5, 6, 7, 8, 9, 11, and 12.
Andrew wrote chapters 1, 2, 3, 4, 10, and 13.

Introduction

From Andrew: A few years ago, I was asked to speak on the subject of "Teaching Psalms to Teens." As I prepared for that lesson, I was reminded of the range of emotions revealed in the psalms. The psalms show the psalmist at the height of joy and praise ("I love the Lord because He hears my voice and my supplications" Psalm 116:1), or at the depth of grief and despair ("I have become like a man without strength, forsaken among the dead..." Psalm 88:4-5).

As I thought back to my own teen years, I remembered the roller-coaster of emotions we all experience during that time. The book of Psalms reminds us that human beings have always dealt with highs and lows, and God remains constant through it all. The psalms give us tools to deal with those challenges, and a better understanding of them can help teens grow and mature through them. It is my prayer that this study guide will help teens grow in faith through their school years.

This book is dedicated to my wife, Kathryn, who has been a constant encourager for me, and to my sons, Luke and Micah, who teach me more than they realize.

From James: Psalms is a big book because it deals with big themes. It would take more than a few pages to describe God's work in creation, His presence in our past, present, and future, His endless love, and His terrifying wrath. But it's all there. Psalms also points the reader to Jesus through many prophecies, and it shows us how man is totally dependent upon God and the work of His Son for salvation. So, it is good for teenagers to study Psalms. They need to learn to think big spiritually. Teenagers tend to minimize God, sin, salvation, and, quite frankly, themselves. Psalms expands their minds. Psalm after psalm, David and others, through inspiration of the Holy Spirit, paint a beautiful picture of how the all-powerful God loves His ever-failing creation. It is my prayer that this book helps young people know and appreciate that love.

Ralph Waldo Emerson wrote, "Our chief want is someone who will inspire us to be what we know we could be." Those who have inspired me to write have been my late mother, Dianne Hayes, my father, John Hayes, and many friends and teachers. This book is dedicated to them.

A Word to the Teacher

Each lesson focuses on a specific psalm or psalms. Since there are 150 psalms, it's impossible to cover them all in one thirteen-week study. Thirteen psalms have been selected in order to represent the different types of psalms as well as some of the most well-known psalms. Our hope is that after spending thirteen weeks in this study, teens will have explored the various types of psalms and will have learned how to apply them. Because this book is designed to facilitate a practical discussion of the psalms, you might want to consult a good commentary to explore some of the deeper issues of each one. Since we use several personal illustrations, we've included the name of each chapter's author in the table of contents.

There will be more information, options, and activities than you will have time to explore in a single class session. It's always better to have more material than needed than to finish a lesson and realize there is still time left! Don't worry about covering every single one; pick and choose which activities fit your class and your context. Be sure to use at least one or two of the "Time-Outs," since they're designed to appeal to the various learning styles in your class. In the teacher's guide at the back of the book, there are guidelines for leading each session. Because the psalms were written as songs, each lesson suggests a song to sing at the beginning of class. Many of those songs have lyrics taken directly from the psalm for that lesson. If you would rather use another song, feel free to do it. You know what will work best for your class. Above all, pray about it and be creative. God bless you as you teach His Word.

Chapter 1

Worshipping God

Psalm 150

Psalm Song Suggestion – "Here I Am to Worship"

So, how do you feel about your faith?

I mean, how do you really feel? Not just the answer you think the Bible class teacher wants you to say. Not just the smile you flash when someone at a worship service asks how you are doing and you are too embarrassed to tell the truth. Not just the front you put on for your friends. How do you really feel?

If we're honest, sometimes we feel great about our own faith. Time at a church camp, around God's incredible creation, can help us feel close to Him. Worshipping at a youth rally with hundreds of Christians our age can be awe-inspiring. If you are a Christian, do you remember how you felt right after being baptized? Were you on fire and determined to live for God?

There are other times, though, that we don't feel quite as great. Our schedule gets crowded, and prayer time is one of the first things to disappear. We look at other people who seem to have everything together and feel like we don't quite measure up. We read about people in the Bible like Moses, David, or Paul, incredible examples of faith, and we wonder why we don't feel that way all the time.

That's where the psalms can help us. The psalms prove that followers of God have always dealt with emotional highs and lows. There are moments in the psalms where the psalmist is overwhelmed with joy and cannot believe how much God has blessed him. There are other times, though, that the psalmist is crying out to God in terrible pain, when he feels abandoned and alone in his grief. No matter which way we are feeling, we can find a psalm to help us deal with those emotions. The more we learn about the psalms, the better we'll be able to handle the ups and downs of life.

Time-Out #1

Hand out slips of paper to each student, and ask them to write down a challenge or problem that discourages them in their faith. Then collect the slips of paper and write some of those on the board. Keep a list of these suggestions throughout the study, and when a psalm hits on one of these challenges, let everyone know.

A Worshipful Psalm

It might seem strange to start a study of psalms with the last one in the book, but Psalm 150 brings up an important topic to discuss before getting too deep into the Psalms. It is straightforward, emphasizing praise to God. You probably noticed when reading this psalm that several musical instruments are mentioned: trumpets, harps, lyres, timbrels, stringed instruments, pipes, cymbals, etc. This is not the only psalm that mentions instruments, and it might seem strange to see all the ones listed. It points to the fundamental question of the definition of true worship and causes us to ask ourselves what kind of worship God wants from us today. Before we go any further with the psalms, we need to deal with both of those subjects.

Years ago, I remember being handed a brochure about the way a certain group worshipped. As I read through the material, I noticed a list of the different things they did in worship, with a verse included below each one. When it came to using instruments, the scriptures were from the Old Testament. This was the first time I had seen some of those Old Testament passages, and a few of them were direct quotes from the psalms. You may be in that same situation, seeing some of these things in Psalms for the first time. Or you might have heard them before and have always wondered about using instruments today. To understand how we should worship today, we need to explore those Old Testament passages and think about how to understand them.

Temple Worship

Listen to how the temple worship is described in 2 Chronicles 29:25: "He then stationed the Levites in the house of the LORD with cymbals,

Time-Out #2

Ask for two volunteers from the class – individuals who don't mind being in front of people and possibly doing something a little embarrassing! Set up a table and two bags of marshmallows at the front of the classroom. Have each contestant take the "Marshmallow Challenge!"

with harps and with lyres, according to the command of David and of Gad the king's seer, and of Nathan the prophet; for the command was from the LORD through His prophets." Did you catch that last phrase? The command to use these instruments was from God. Not only were they used in the temple, God also gave specific instructions as to how they should be used. In fact, the Israelites would have been doing wrong if they had decided not to use the instruments in the way God commanded.

When we arrive at the New Testament, we see a contrast between temple worship and Christian worship. The book of Hebrews gives us insight into these differences. It was written to Jewish Christians, who would have been raised under the old covenant but were adjusting to living as Christians under the new covenant. The Israelites had offered animal sacrifices in worship, yet once Jesus came, there was no need for those offerings. The Israelites had been led in worship by priests, but that was not needed after Jesus' sacrifice.

Time Out #3

Have a quick class brainstorming session. What are some laws or practices in the Old Testament that are not carried over into the New Testament? See how many you can think of in three minutes.

To Strike or To Speak?

To help us understand the relationship between the Old and New Testament, let's check out the man who received the Ten Commandments on Mt. Sinai. Numbers 20 gives us an interesting insight into the life of Moses. He had been leading Israel through the wilderness for decades by this point, and he was going through a difficult time. His sister, Miriam, had just died, and the Israelites were complaining about not having any water. Can you imagine how frustrating it would be to deal with the kinds of complaints Moses constantly faced? God gave him clear instructions in verse 8—to take his rod, go with Aaron, and speak to a rock before the Israelites. Water would then come out of the rock. That might seem strange at first, but remember the different ways God was providing for His people during this time. He had parted the waters of the Red Sea to deliver them from Egypt, and He was sending manna (bread from Heaven) and quail for them to eat. In fact, they had already seen water come from a rock. Exodus 17:1-7 tells us that when the Israelites had needed water earlier, Moses had struck a rock and water came forth.

That was not, however, what God commanded in Numbers 20. He told Moses to speak to the rock. Yet when Moses went to the rock, with the rod in his hand, he said to Israel, "Listen now, you rebels; shall we bring forth water for you out of this rock?" (vs. 10). Then he struck the rock with his rod. Water still came out of the rock. God still took care of His people who needed water. But something was wrong; Moses had not followed God's instructions. He had claimed partial credit for the miracle ("Shall *we* bring forth water out of this rock?"), and he had struck it rather than speak to it. Numbers 20:12 tells us that Moses had to face the consequences. That decision cost Moses the chance to set foot in Canaan, the Promised Land. Moses had been leading the Israelites toward that goal for decades, but he would not be able to enjoy it.

But what does this story from the life of Moses have to do with worship? It illustrates an important principle. The first time around, God gave him a specific instruction: Strike the rock. Moses did it. The second time around, God gave Moses a different instruction: speak to the rock. He didn't tell Moses not to strike it because he didn't need to strike it. He had given him a different command. When we picture Moses striking the rock in Numbers 20, we all recognize the disobedience. In the Old Testament, God had specific instructions for worship that involved animal sacrifices, musical instruments, and priests in the temple. In the New Testament, God gives different instructions. Sacrifices, animals, and the priestly duties that we read about in the Old Testament aren't mentioned. Rather than offering animal sacrifices, we are called to be baptized to be cleansed by the blood of Jesus, our ultimate sacrifice. We are commanded to worship God by singing, praying, studying His Word, observing the Lord's Supper, and giving back to God. There is no group of people designated to be priests who make sacrifices, but in a way, all Christians are "priests." We can talk to God in prayer, and we offer ourselves as living sacrifices.

We need to think carefully about the story of Moses. When it comes to worship, we need to do what God has told us in the New Testament. Just because something used to be part of serving God under the Old Covenant doesn't mean we should bring it into the New Covenant.

Giving a Gift

What happens when you're buying someone a birthday present? If that person is important to you, you'll probably search for exactly the right gift. You'll ask around to find out what that person might want before you go shopping. If it's a piece of clothing, you will want to figure out what the right size would be and what color your friend would like best. Even if it's a gift card, you will want to find the right store, restaurant, or website. When we care about people and want to give them something, we look for what they want. If we love God and want to show Him worship, then shouldn't we give Him what He wants? What if your friend did not enjoy sports at all, but you gave him tickets to see a local baseball team play because you like baseball? How do you think that gift would be received?

That example may be extreme, but isn't that what happens when we make decisions about worship based only on what we like? If God describes the worship He wants from us in the New Testament, why would we want to add to those guidelines or substitute our own ideas? Both the Old and New Testaments remind us that our priority in worship is to glorify God, not to serve ourselves. That means the standard for a good worship service isn't that we "got something out of it," although we will be blessed by worshipping. The standard is whether or not we glorified God according to His Word. The way we honor God is by giving Him what He has requested in worship. If we think about everything He has done for us, we realize that we could never repay Him for our blessings. That leads us to constant praise, just like the kind we see in Psalm 150.

Time Out #4

Take a few minutes to read and think about these statements; what do they tell us about common attitudes in worship? How should we respond to these thoughts in a godly way?

- "I just didn't get much out of the worship service this morning."
- "I don't really like the songs we sang today. It was hard for me to get into worship."
- "The service was pretty boring. It was hard to focus."

Putting It All Together

1. When people ask us how we are doing, we are usually tempted to say we are doing fine, even when we aren't. Why is it difficult to admit to someone else when things aren't going well in life?
2. How could reading the psalms help you when you are facing a challenge to your faith?

3. Can you imagine being in Moses' place in Numbers 20? Have you ever said something you shouldn't have because you were upset?

4. Based on the passages we've studied, what are the qualities of "good worship?"

5. Can you think of a time in life when you were overwhelmed with joy and just wanted to praise God the way the psalmist does in Psalm 150?

Taking It Home

Choose at least two psalms to read some time during the week. After reading them, stop and think about the ways they reflect challenges in your own life.

Chapter 2

Introducing the Psalms

Psalms 1-2

Psalm Song Suggestion – "Step by Step"

All of us have pet peeves, little things in life that annoy us. One of mine is missing the first few minutes of a movie or TV show. I like to have all the information about the plot and characters and be prepared for whatever happens. I don't like picking up halfway through the movie and trying to figure out what's happening. If I'm flipping through the channels and land in the middle of a movie that I've wanted to see, I'll take the remote and keep going. If I want to watch it, I'll come back and watch the entire movie from the beginning. This is also why I don't like being late to see a movie in the theater (although the previews last a long time).

You can tell a lot about a movie by the opening scene. It usually shows you who the main character is or what the plot is going to be. An action movie might start with the background of the hero, showing the situation that reveals the motivation behind a hero's actions. A romantic comedy will probably begin by showing the main characters in their natural environment so the audience can get a sense of their personalities. There might be a sweeping camera shot of a city skyline to give you a sense of where it takes place, or it might open up in the interior of a house, to let you know a little about the characters' lives. You can count on the fact that the director has put serious thought into how the film opens, so that it will strike just the right note. However a movie starts, making that first scene grab the audience's attention is a big deal.

As the book of Psalms begins, the first two psalms do the same thing as an opening movie scene. They set the stage for what the book is going to be about and the major themes we will see. Just like we don't want to be late to a movie because we might miss out on important information, we don't need to start a study of Psalms without focusing on Psalms 1 and 2. They set the tone for the purpose of the book, and they show the poetic style of writing that extends through every psalm. These psalms hold up God's wisdom and signal that the psalms in this book are going to promote godly wisdom.

Practical Poetry

When Jesus starts the Sermon on the Mount in Matthew 5, He begins with what we usually call the "Beat-itudes." Those statements begin with "Blessed are…" and then describe the kind of people who are doing things that might not always seem popular (mourning, showing mercy, seeking peace) but are spiritually valuable in God's eyes. Psalm 1 begins in the same way, describing the blessings that come when someone refuses to walk with people who are doing wicked things, stand with people doing sinful things, or sit with people mocking what is good. There are actually twenty-five different beatitude statements in the Psalms, and the next one comes at the end of Psalm 2. Psalm 2:12 states that all who take refuge in the Lord will be blessed. Of course, each psalm can stand on its own, but these two seem to fit closely together.

These "blessed are" statements remind us that these psalms weren't intended only to be beautiful poems that were read, talked about for a few minutes, and then put back on the shelf. They are great works of poetry, but are also much more. They're intended to instruct us on how to live. In that sense, the psalms are like practical poetry. After all, these were the songs sung by God's people. Whether it's in a Sunday morning worship service or a weekend devotional, when we sing praise, we aren't just singing a melo-

Time Out #1

Memorizing passages from the psalms might not be as hard as you think. Take a few minutes to list some of your favorite devotional songs. Try to think of songs taken from passages in Psalms. There is a list in the back of the book, if you need help getting started. You might be surprised to see how many verses of the psalms you've already committed to memory.

Time-Out #2

Look at the list of worship songs you made earlier. Pick out two or three and recite the words. What do those songs teach? Can you think of a time when you sang one of them without really reflecting on what the song meant? How can Christians avoid that temptation?

dy that sounds good or words that seem nice. In Colossians 3:16, Paul told the Christians in Colosse that when they sang "psalms, hymns, or spiritual songs," they weren't only praising God, they were also teaching one another.

A Different Beat

You may have heard the description of a person who stands out from the crowd as someone who "marches to the beat of a different drum." I didn't fully understand what that meant until my sophomore year in high school. I played the saxophone in our school band, at least until my sophomore year. Because we only had one percussionist that year, I was recruited to play percussion on a few songs. The percussion section was in the back of the band, and since I hadn't played percussion before, I had a lot to learn. This was all new to me, and I would get so focused on making sure I was reading the music and hitting the right notes that I would forget to look up. There were times when I looked up at our band director to see him glaring at me, because I was no longer following him.

It was important for the percussion section to follow the conductor. Drums are loud, and if they're at a different pace than everyone else, it's easy for the entire band to play at the drum's tempo instead of sticking with the director. As the psalmist describes a follower of God, he writes about someone who refuses to be led by anyone else.

Psalm 1 begins by describing someone who has chosen the right way to live—refusing to walk with people who do wicked things, to stand with people who do sinful things, or to sit with people who mock what is good. The idea of choosing the right way is a theme that stretches throughout the Bible. Psalm 1 also warns against allowing other people to influence us. He refers to the "wicked," (lawless people who make up their own rules) "sinners," (people who constantly disobey God), and "scoffers" (cynical people who constantly make fun of righteous things).

You've probably been advised how important the choices are that you're making in your lives right now. The decisions about the friends you make, who you will date, what you will do for a living, etc. are all incredibly important. The people with whom you spend time will affect who you become as you mature. The things you choose to do now will affect how you think about life. What kind of person will you be? You'll probably be a lot like your friends with whom you spend time each day. How will you think? Your thinking will be shaped and molded by what you watch and read.

18

Time-Out #3

As a class, brainstorm a list of real-life situations in which teens are tempted to hang out with people who are doing things that are wrong or are making fun of others. Try to come up with at least three different scenarios, and then divide into three groups. Assign each group one of the situations, and then give them 3-4 minutes to decide how a Christian should respond. A spokesperson for each group can share the results with the class. Be sure to explore the consequences of each action and think through what the effects would be.

Who Is In Power?

Psalm 2 moves from a focus on a righteous individual to an entire nation. Psalm 2 is often called a "royal psalm," because it focuses on the role of the king. Throughout the psalm, we're reminded that God's wisdom and power are far above the abilities of earthly leaders. In Acts 4, after Peter and John are arrested and led before the Sanhedrin because they were preaching about Jesus, they quoted this psalm. It's a reminder that God is ultimately the One in control.

This would have been important for Israel, because they often had to deal with opposing nations waging war. Verse 2 states that these enemies are "devising" against God's people. This indicates serious plotting; Israel had enemies that were carefully designing battle plans to war against them. When we watch war movies, we usually see "war rooms" where the army leaders gather. There are maps on the wall; computers and monitors abound and receive a steady stream of important information. Generals carefully map out a strategy for the impending battle. Psalm 2 paints this kind of picture, but then describes God's reaction. When enemies band together, God laughs. Even the best battle plans don't faze the Creator of the world.

This is important to remember, because it's easy to lose sight of God's power. All of us, on some level, care about what other people think. We want to impress people who are popular and have a lot of influence over others. We want people to like us: to invite us to hang out with them, to think that our clothes look good, and to think they were fun to have as friends. We worry about what they think, even when we're making small decisions. If someone insults us or makes fun of us, we can allow those things to have a serious effect. Yet if we remember that God's power is greater than anyone else's, we can have a different perspective. Paul would put it this way in Romans 8:31: "If God is for us, who is against us?" Though it still hurts when we don't get the acceptance or support that we might want, it helps to know that God's opinion is ultimately the one that matters.

King of Kings

This psalm focuses on the "Lord's anointed," which is a reference to the King of Israel. When God chose a king, that person would be anointed. Both Saul and David were anointed by Samuel to indicate that God had chosen them to be king. Like many of the psalms, descriptions of an earthly king are also used to describe Jesus. In Acts 13:33, Paul uses a line from this psalm— "You are my Son; today I have begotten You"—to describe Jesus. Just as our Heavenly Father chose the King of Israel (as the original audience of Psalm 2 would have understood it), the Heavenly Father sent the Son into the world. The book of Hebrews uses the same passage twice to emphasize that Jesus is the Son of God (1:5, 5:5).

The other nations in the psalm are urged to recognize God's authority and worship Him in reverence. The language used carries with it the idea of service. Verse 12 states that they should also honor the King that God appointed. For the Israelites, people who wanted to honor God needed to honor the earthly king. For us, if we want to honor God, then we must honor Jesus. In Philippians 2, Paul reminds us of this principle. In Verses 9-11, he writes: "Therefore God has highly exalted him (Jesus) and bestowed on him the name that is above every name, so that at the name of Jesus every knee should bow, in heaven and on earth and under the earth, and every tongue confess that Jesus Christ is Lord, to the glory of God the Father." (ESV) We cannot serve God without honoring Jesus. When we do both, as both Psalm 1 and Psalm 2 tell us, we will be blessed.

Time-Out #4

Since you have started thinking about songs taken from the psalms, this would be a good time to write a psalm as a class. Take a few minutes for each person to think of a phrase that praises God. Put them all together, and see if you can put them to a familiar tune (the tune of *Amazing Grace* works with just about anything).

Putting It All Together

1. What can we learn about the book of Psalms by reading these first two psalms?
2. In what ways do Christians live differently than those around them? What are the challenges that come with those differences?
3. Psalm 1 describes a faithful person as a tree planted by the water. What can we learn about the blessings of faithful living from that image?
4. How does it make you feel to know that God is far more powerful than any enemy we might have?
5. In what ways does our world dishonor Jesus? How can we set an example of honoring Jesus?

Bringing It Home

This week, find a way to honor Jesus. Maybe you can have a discussion with a friend at school about why Jesus matters to you. You might be able to do something nice for others, and when they ask you why, explain that you're a Christian. Always be searching for ways to honor the Father and the Son.

Chapter 3

In the Beginning...

Psalm 8

Psalm Song Suggestion – "O Lord, Our Lord, How Majestic Is Your Name"

Time Out #1

At the beginning of class, fill a box with all kinds of random, everyday objects. Allow each class member to have exactly sixty seconds to look at all the objects in the box. Make sure everyone is silent during this time, just trying to remember all the objects. Take the next few minutes to sing "O Lord, Our Lord, How Majestic Is Your Name In all the Earth," "Majestic," or another song about God's glory in creation. After that, have everyone write down all the objects they can remember, and see who can remember the most. The person who remembers the most gets a prize – something from the box (teacher's choice).

Mountaintop Experiences

Can you think of a time when you felt close to God? Visualize that time in your mind; did it happen at a retreat or church camp? I will never forget some of the devotionals that took place with my youth group during retreats: sitting around a bonfire, singing songs of praise, eating lunch while looking at an incredible forest. Those activities put us in a frame of mind to praise God. There's something about being close to nature that causes us to feel closer to God, and that feeling is nothing new.

Even in the Old Testament, followers of God were inspired by creation. In many ways, ancient cultures were more dependent on the natural world than we are today. Their farming kept them dependent on the land. Their reliance on rain for their crops made them pay attention to the weather patterns. Their care for flocks of sheep and herds of cattle taught them about God's design. We see this focus on creation several times in the psalms. Psalm 8 is sometimes called a "creation psalm." There are several of these, including 19, 33, 89, 104, and 148. Not only do they focus on God's work in creation, they also view it as motivation to worship. Read Psalm 8 together as a class, and look for what it tells us about creation.

The Name of the Lord

You probably noticed that the first and last verses begin with the same phrase: "O Lord, our Lord, how majestic is your name in all the earth." It's almost like the two verses work as bookends, tying the psalm together. From the beginning of this psalm to the end, the name of the Lord is praised. The psalms often use repetition to drive a point home, but there is another reason why we read the name "Lord" twice in our English versions. The first is the covenant name of God, the one we usually pronounce "Yahweh." We don't know exactly how to pronounce it, because the Israelites considered this special name so holy that they would not say it out loud. Compare that to how many times we hear God's name used in vain today. This special name is the beginning of the psalm, and then a more general name for "lord" (which means "master") is used. In other words, the God of the Israelites is our master.

The psalmist goes on to say that the Lord's name is majestic in all the earth. In order to understand why this phrase is so important, we need to know how the ancient Israelites viewed names. They looked at names in a different way than we do. For them, the meaning of a name was incredibly important. For example, John the Baptist was given his name by God. "John" means "favored of God." Another man we read about in the Old Testament was named "Nabal," which means "fool." Can you imagine your parents giving you that kind of name?

As followers of God, we carry the name of Christ. This name describes the Savior whom God promised in the Old Testament. The term means "anointed one," and God sent His Son Jesus to this earth as the anointed One. That is why we usually think of His name this way—Jesus Christ. It isn't the last name of Jesus; it is a description of Jesus' identity as the Savior. In Acts

Time Out #2

Think of something in nature that reminds you of God, either because of its appearance, its design, or any other reason. Share it with the class, along with the reason why you chose it. If the weather is nice enough, you can even have the students take a walk outside and choose something.

11:26, we see the church in Antioch is where followers of Christ were first called "Christians." It is not the only name used in the Bible for the church; Christians are also referred to as disciples and those belonging to The Way, for example. But the term "Christian" is the most common one used today. It reminds us that we are to be representatives of Christ, the anointed one.

There's another way we see the concept of "the name" in Scripture. The "name" refers to an extension of someone's identity and reputation. By saying that God's name is exalted all over the earth, the psalmist is saying that people find out about God from all over His creation. Paul made this

Time Out #3

Divide the class into three groups, and assign each group one of these passages: Genesis 17:1-6, Genesis 32:24-28, and Matthew 16:16-20. Each text describes a follower of God whose name is changed, and after that change is a reason for the new name. After reading the passage together, each group should answer these questions: Who has his name changed in this passage? What did that change mean? End this time by discussing how God has changed our name to "Christian," indicating our mission for Him.

same point in Romans 1:20, writing "For since the creation of the world His invisible attributes, His eternal power and divine nature, have been clearly seen, being understood through what has been made, so that they are without excuse." Wherever we look around us, we see evidence of the One who created our world.

Creation

When we read descriptions of creation in the psalms, we should remember what kind of writing we're reading. It's not designed to be scientifically technical, but poetic. A few years ago, my wife and I visited Volcanoes National Park in Hilo, Hawaii. We started our journey in the park museum, and we walked through displays of geological overlays and diagrams of the different layers of earth and technical descriptions of how the volcano formed. Then, we walked into a small theater and watched actual footage of the last time the volcano erupted. The announcer described what we were seeing: lava spewing out the top and flowing across the surface and smoke rising from the top. Even if you closed your eyes and just listened to his description, you could envision every detail. Those were two explanations of a volcano: a technical diagram and a vivid description. Both were accurate, but they were different. When we read the books of history in the Old Testament, we get a technical, accurate description of history. When we read the psalms, we usually get that second kind of description—words that paint pictures.

Even in a time before telescopes and satellites, people were amazed by the sun, moon, and stars. The scientifically technical facts we know about the sun, moon, and stars are impressive enough. Our earth is located just the right distance from the sun—far enough away so that we don't burn up, yet close enough that our planet can sustain life. Our tides are controlled by the gravitational pull of the moon as it relates to the earth. The more we discover about our world, the clearer it is that God designed it especially for human life. Although the psalmist didn't have the technical knowledge of the 21st century, he did know the other kind of information—the beauty of creation. Other ancient cultures worshipped the sun or moon, but the psalmist knew better. He knew that the true God created those things.

Mankind

I had never felt that way before in my life. We had just left the delivery room and entered the hospital nursery. Since there were several new arrivals that morning, the nurse rushed off to help with another delivery, leaving me alone in the nursery, looking at my newborn son. When I reflect on that moment, I can't remember a specific feeling. What comes to mind is an overwhelming mixture of emotions—love, joy, relief, excitement, and anxiety, to name a few. As I signaled to family members through the glass window and watched my son lying there, one word described the experience—amazing. If you've ever seen a newborn baby, you know the feeling. You see the tiny fingers and toes, listen to the voice crying, and realize the incredible nature of God's creation. Three years later, when our second son was born, the emotions were every bit as overwhelming. It's this kind of feeling the psalmist describes in Psalm 8.

This psalm highlights God's creation in several different ways. Verse 2 mentions the strength of God established in infants. That may seem strange, because we know that babies are weak, depending on adults to take care of them. Yet, even in this form, a human being is evidence of God's intricate design. We're also reminded in verses 6-8 that God has given man dominion over creation. Even in the beginning, Adam was the one who had the authority to name all the animals. In Genesis 1:28, we see that God designed man to rule over the earth, to subdue it, and to rule over the animals.

We also know from Genesis 1:27 that we are made in the image of God. In another psalm, we read that we are "formed by God" and "fearfully and wonderfully made" (Psalm 139:13-14). Think about that. When you see a kid at school who's ridiculed, that is a person made in the image of God. When you look at someone in the youth group who gets under your skin, that is a person made in the image of God. When you look in the mirror and find fault with the way you look, remember that you are made in the image of God. We can probably all think of things about ourselves we would like to change, but we need to remember we're fearfully and wonderfully made. There may even be other kids at school who give you a hard time or spread embarrassing rumors about you. Before you get down on yourself, remember whose image you bear.

Time Out #4

The things we tell ourselves (sometimes called "self-talk") are important. As a class, make a list of all the negative messages we're tempted to tell ourselves about our physical appearance – that we aren't attractive enough, athletic enough, etc. Put all those on one side of the board. On the other side, write out this phrase – "I am fearfully and wonderfully made." As a class, read together each statement on the left side, followed by the phrase "I am fearfully and wonderfully made." The next time you're tempted to give yourself a negative message, remember this powerful fact from Scripture.

Putting It All Together

1. We began class by discussing how the busy nature of life can crowd out our relationship with God. What can we do to reserve time to spend in God's Word and prayer?

2. Psalm 8 reminds us of the importance of God's name. How do you hear God's name taken in vain today? What should we do when we hear God's name taken in vain?

3. How should someone act who wears the name of Christ?

4. Why do you think our society is fixated on image? What does it mean to be made in the image of God?

5. How does it make you feel to know that you are fearfully and wonderfully made by God?

Taking It Home

This week, take some time to read one of these creation psalms: 19, 33, 89, 104, or 148. Do you notice any similarities between that psalm and Psalm 8? What does it teach us about God's creation? Spend time in prayer, thanking God for the world He has given us.

Chapter 4

Weathering the Storm

Psalm 13
Psalm Song Suggestion – Hide Me Away, Oh Lord

Weather Patterns

When I was in college, a group of us spent six weeks in Thailand as part of a mission trip. At one point, four of us were in a small boat, headed across an inlet of the Indian Ocean to meet with a congregation for Sunday morning worship. Though it wasn't a long boat ride, there was a point where we were too far away from the shore to see land. That's when I noticed storm clouds forming. Waves began to rock the boat a little bit, and we felt the rain begin to fall. What began as a simple, calm boat ride had quickly turned into something else. I still remember sitting in that boat, wondering what was going to happen. I knew how to swim, and I had a life jacket on, but I was gripping my backpack and looking around, planning what I would do in case of an emergency. Which shoreline was the closest? How could I get there? Our experienced boat driver, however, wasn't worried at all. We made it to the other side without any problems. Even though we weren't in any real danger, the sudden storm definitely got our attention! That can happen with weather, can't it? In the blink of an eye, things can change.

When we think of psalms, we usually picture beautiful poetry. We think of calm, smooth waters. We imagine a shepherd sitting under a tree, with the sun in the sky and a gentle breeze coming off a stream. As he enjoys the shade, he plays the harp and reflects on God's creation. We think about words of praise, repeated like the chorus of a song. You might even recognize that some of our devotional songs are taken directly from the words of the Psalms. Psalms are often associated with peaceful scenes of pastures and sheep. That isn't a bad thing, but we would be mistaken if we thought those were the only psalms in the book.

Just like our weather patterns, the climate for the psalmist isn't always calm and breezy. In fact, there are many times in the psalms where the writer faces severe weather: vicious enemies, intense pain, blinding confusion. These psalms are anything but peaceful. They are often referred to as "laments." In a lament psalm, the writer asks questions so difficult that you can practically hear the pain in his voice. Questions like, "Why, Lord?" and "How long?" are common, as the psalmist lays out his pain before God.

These psalms aren't necessarily optimistic, but they are important. They're important because life isn't always calm. Sometimes the weather gets rough. The death of someone important in your life leaves you in the fog of grief. The bitter words of someone at school can inflict a stinging pain that makes you dread going back the next day. The person you thought would always be your best friend starts to change, and you wonder who will fill that role in your life. All those events can leave you reeling, wondering if anyone truly cares.

Time-Out #1

Think about some tough times Christians face. They don't have to be personal, although you can share some of those if you'd like. What are some questions Christians ask during that time? Make a list. Why might Christians sometimes be afraid to ask those questions?

How Long?

Like many of the lament psalms, you can feel the emotions of the psalmist from the beginning. The first questions plead with God, asking how long God will hide His face from the psalmist. God seems distant, and the psalmist feels miserable day and night. Think about the last time you were sick and had to stay in bed for one or two days. Even when you get back to your normal schedule, you may still feel bad for a day or so. It's miserable to try to go to school or work a job when you feel sick. Imagine if your miserable feeling didn't go away after a few days. If you can picture that, you can envision the pain of the psalmist.

How long? That's the question we ask, isn't it? How many more mornings do we have to endure those kids making fun of us before it is over? How much more pain do we have to feel before the problems at home are solved? Psalm 13 asks the same question. He asks how long God will be removed from his life, and he asks how long his enemy will be victorious. Everything was falling apart, yet he turned to God. His challenges, as difficult as they might have been, didn't cause him to stop believing in God altogether. One thing all these laments have in common is that they're addressed to God. They might question God's actions or His justice, but they don't question God's existence. They still look to Him for answers.

The Value of Lament

This psalm reminds us is it isn't wrong to ask God tough questions. During the times when we struggle with our faith, we may be afraid to say out loud what's bothering us. Can you think of times you've been reluctant to admit how you were feeling in prayer to God? Have you ever been angry about something that happened, but you were worried that telling God about it would be like you were angry with Him? Have you ever been grieving over a loss, but you were worried that telling God about your shock and confusion would be like saying you didn't trust Him?

Sometimes, we think that if we admit to facing challenges, we'll become "inferior" Christians, but that isn't what this psalm teaches. We can express our mixed emotions and our difficult feelings to God. After all, He already knows what we're thinking. Do we really believe we can hide our thoughts and feelings from Him? We won't surprise God, but we might be surprised at how much better we feel after we pray openly and honestly to Him.

Recently, I accidentally got two fingers of my left hand caught in the hinges of a door as it closed. If that's ever happened to you, you know the kind of sudden pain that shoots through your hand. I was in the lobby of a building, and I needed to get to my car, make the short ride home, and put some ice on my fingers. Though I was in pain, what I did next was interesting. Instinctively, I pretended that it hadn't really hurt. I assured the people near me that I was fine and it wasn't a big deal, even though it was all I could do to keep from yelling in pain. I waved to everyone and walked calmly to my car.

Why do we do that? Why do we act like we're fine when we're in pain? Why do we talk to our friends in Bible class like we have no problems, even though we're hurting inside? Why do we expend so much energy trying to act like everything is great when it isn't? More importantly, why would we try to do that before God? Why would we pretend like nothing is wrong before the One who knows everything?

Job and His Questions

It's difficult to think about a psalm like this without remembering Job in the Old Testament. Even if you've never read the book of Job, you're probably heard of him. His name has become a synonym for suffering. When we're introduced to him in Job 1, we find out he is a blameless and upright servant of

Time-Out #2

You may have heard people refer to the grieving process. Researchers like Elisabeth Kubler-Ross have pointed to specific phases of grief that occur when someone experiences loss. Though these stages don't always occur in this specific order, many believe people who are grieving have to work through anger, bargaining, and depression before they can reach acceptance. Counselors often encourage people to keep journals recording how they feel, which can help them process these emotions in a healthy way. These lament psalms show us that we have only discovered what God already knew – human beings need to work through these difficult emotions, and it takes time. God created us, and He knows how our emotions work better than anyone else. Lament psalms show us how followers of God worked through difficult times while staying faithful. They can be a model for us today.

God. Satan comes to God and offers a challenge—if you take away all of Job's blessings, then he will turn his back on you. God gives Satan permission to do just that. Satan takes away everything Job has and gives him painful sores. The only living family member Job has left is his wife, who encourages Job to curse God and die (not a great encouragement for Job to hold on to faith).

Here is the interesting thing: that all happens within the first two chapters of the book. In the last chapter, God rewards Job for his faithfulness. Have you ever stopped to read all those chapters in between? Job has a long discussion with his friends about his situation that results in a direct message from God Himself. Much of what Job says in those chapters sounds like Psalm 13; he asks some tough questions. He questions why God is causing him to suffer. He asks what he did wrong, and claims that he is innocent. His friends counter all those questions with a simple explanation: Job must have sinned and brought all these bad things on himself. Job disagrees.

Then comes the interesting part;

though God rewards Job in chapter 42, He is not happy with Job's friends. In verse 8, He tells them that they needed to take seven bulls and seven rams to Job and ask him to offer a sacrifice on their behalf. He follows that with this statement—"Because you have not spoken of Me what is right, as My servant Job has." They claimed to have all the answers, and Job asked hard questions. In the end, they were the ones who were mistaken. Job was honest with God about his pain, which tells us that we can be honest about our pain as well.

Ending With Praise

One of the features of this psalm that may seem strange is that the

Time-Out #3

Divide into two groups. The first group has a simple task: list individuals in Scripture who endured serious suffering and remained faithful. Have one person in that group write down the names of each person and a short sentence describing what that person endured. The second group has a similar task: list people they know who have endured serious suffering and remained faithful to God. Have one person in that group write down the information as well, and then compare notes.

psalmist ends on a positive note. He has just listed all the different struggles he has, and he has lamented his state in life, yet he ends by praising God. That's something we see in many of the lament psalms; they might start out negative, but they often end on a positive note of praising God. Because Psalm 13 is one of the shortest psalms in the book, this transition is a little more noticeable. At the end of Psalm 13, the psalmist concludes with trusting in the Lord's love and salvation. In verse 6, he sings to the Lord, because the Lord has dealt bountifully with him.

How is this possible? How can someone go from bitterly complaining to praising God? Verse 5 tells us how—he trusted in what he already knew about God. When he said the Lord had dealt bountifully with him, he is referring to blessings that he had already been given. He could look back in his life and see all the different ways God had blessed him. James 1:17 reminds us that every good and perfect gift comes from God. That means that whatever we have that is good is a gift from God. None of his blessings were of his own doing; they were all from God.

He also knew what God had done for his people over the years. He could have paused to remember the way God delivered the Israelites from slavery.

He could have thought back to all the battles against larger, more powerful armies where God granted the victory to Israel. He might simply have reflected on the world around him and remembered that God blessed him with an incredible world where he could live. God's blessings in the past helped him face an uncertain future.

The same thing can work for us. When you come home after a rough day, and it feels like all of life is against you, it is hard to know how to react. Taking a few minutes to think about God's blessings can help us deal with those tough issues. If you're having issues with your friends, you can remember that those friends are blessings from God, and he has given you many fun times together. If you're feeling down or discouraged, remember some of the good days you've experienced. You haven't always felt this way, and you won't feel like this forever. Remembering the past can give you strength for the future.

Putting It Together

1. Do you think lament is helpful? Why or why not?

2. How does it make you feel to read lament psalms?

3. How do these psalms help us relate to the psalmist and his feelings toward God?

4. What could Job's friends have done to be more helpful to him? How can we learn from their example to help us comfort our friends?

5. Why did God preserve lament psalms for us to read?

Time Out #4

After all these hard questions, this psalm ends in praise. Even when we're hurting, we have reasons to praise God. Write on an index card, at least three things for which you can praise God, even when things aren't going well. Put the card in your wallet, purse, or backpack and keep it with you this week.

Bringing It Home

Your challenge this week is to take your index card and spend time praising God for those things this week, even when you're having a bad day or are dealing with a frustrating situation.

Chapter 5

God's Laws vs. Man's Laws

Psalm 19

Psalm Song Suggestion—"Thy Word"

A mechanical wristwatch seems like a simple device since it's only keeping time, but if you look closer, a wristwatch is a complicated timepiece. Behind the face are tiny wheels, screws, and bolts working in perfect harmony to keep the hour, minute, and second hands moving correctly. The face often has more than just numbers on it; there are words and weather images. It's covered by a small piece of glass or clear plastic, and an elastic band attaches to the face so that the wearer can put the watch on the wrist.

Considering that a wristwatch is so complicated, you would assume that somebody designed it. Even though you did not see the watch being made, you know that somewhere, somebody made that watch for the purpose of telling time. We can look at God's creation the same way. This is called the *design argument* for the existence of God. When we see how complex nature is and when we marvel at how our body parts function perfectly together, we cannot help but conclude that somebody must have designed this world and given it a purpose, even though we weren't there to see it being made.

Psalm 19 establishes two fundamental facts about God: First, nature proves that God is real, and second, His Word brought nature into existence and continues to guide men.

Hebrew Poetry

When we read poetry, we often expect it to rhyme or tell a story. Ancient Hebrew poetry, which is what Psalms represents, doesn't rhyme, and it usually doesn't tell a story. (The book of Job and parts of wisdom literature are the exceptions to this style.) The primary purpose of Hebrew poetry was to emphasize godly truths by having each line connect in some way to the

Time Out #1

The design argument is a powerful way to see evidence for the existence of God. Years ago, Antony Flew was one of the world's most famous atheist philosophers. In 1976, he joined in a public debate with Thomas B. Warren, a preacher and teacher, about the existence of God. Flew was involved in several different discussions over the years, and he wrote many articles defending his position. But in 2004, something interesting happened. In an interview, Antony Flew stated "the most impressive arguments for God's existence were related to recent scientific discoveries." Because of what science discovered about human genetics, he began to believe in a designer. In 2007, he published a book entitled *There Is a God*, which stated the reversal of his position. He didn't convert to Christianity, but he changed his mind on the existence of a creator because of design. What are some other ways we see evidence of God's design?

next line. Psalm 19 is a good example of this type of poetic structure.

In verse one, we see the word "telling" followed in the next line with the word "declaring." Repeating the same thought highlights David's point. The second line in verse 10 intensifies the truth being presented: "They are more desirable than gold, yes, than much fine gold." Another way Hebrew poetry highlights truths is by answering a question. Verse 12 states, "Who can discern his errors? Acquit me of hidden faults." So, when you read the poetry and wisdom sections of the Old Testament—Job, Psalms, Proverbs, Ecclesiastes, and Song of Solomon—don't expect the verses to rhyme. Read them as you would any other section of the Bible.

Even Though It Doesn't Have a Mouth, It Can Still Speak

Psalm 19 begins with a dramatic expression: "The heavens are telling of the glory of God; and their expanse is declaring the work of His hands. Day to day pours forth speech, and night to night reveals knowledge" (vs. 1-2).

What does David, the author of this psalm, mean when he writes that the heavens and the days are talking? After all, they don't have a voice or a language. Well, just because something doesn't have a vocabulary doesn't mean it cannot teach us something. In Hebrews 11, we are told that even though Abel, the brother of Cain, was dead, he could still speak (Hebrews 11:4).

The word *heavens* reminds us of Genesis 1:1 when God created the "heavens and the earth." Later we read that the heavens were the space between the water above us (clouds) and the water on earth (seas). (*Heavens* appears about 400 times in the Old Testament.) So the heavens are essentially the atmosphere in which we live. When we see the word *heaven* we instantly think of our eternal home after we die, but that isn't the heaven being addressed in Psalm 19. That heaven is primarily discussed in the New Testament.

David knew the heavens spoke. He spent many days and nights underneath the expanse of the sky when he was a shepherd boy. He saw the clear blue days and the starry nights. He watched the seasons change and the clouds roll. He couldn't help but marvel at the work of God's hands. He undoubtedly wondered why the stars never moved and why the moon changed shape. His scientific knowledge was limited, but he couldn't deny what he was learning from the heavens above him. He knew that God put it all in place. The heavens were speaking to him even though, as he states in 19:3, "There is no speech, nor are there words; their voice is not heard."

God's Laws

In 1961, Alan Shepard became the first American to travel into space. Prior to entering the capsule for that flight, a reporter asked him, "What is the one thing you're depending on most during this space venture?" He said, "I'm depending on the fact that God's laws never change." It would have been impossible for Shepard or any astronaut to travel into space if the laws of science were constantly changing. But Shepard trusted the unchangeable laws of God for his success.

Verse seven states: "The law of the LORD is perfect, restoring the soul; the testimony of the LORD is sure, making wise the simple." God made the world exactly the way He wanted to make it. Throughout the days of creation, God declared that what He had made was good (Genesis 1:10, 12, 17, 21, and 25). After the sixth day, "God saw all that He had made, and behold, it was very good" (Genesis 1:31). The crowning work of His creation was man, who was made in God's image. Since the all-powerful, all-knowing God made this world and all things in it exactly how He wanted to make it, we can assume that anything else that originates with God is good for us. That includes His laws.

If you take a typical King James Bible (not a study Bible) and open it in the middle, you will probably open to the book of Psalms, and you will probably be near Psalm 119. It is the longest chapter in the Bible. It is divided into eight-verse segments, with each segment designated with a different letter of the Hebrew alphabet. So what do you think is the one topic that is addressed in Psalm 119? The law of God. Through the providence and the inspiration of the Holy Spirit, the longest chapter of the Bible could have been about love, joy, compassion, prayer, or any other major Bible doctrine. But no. It's about the joy that comes from following the perfect laws of God.

Time Out #2

This psalm reminds us of the power of God's Word, which is a theme that surfaces often in the Bible. Read the following description of God's Word, which is taken from a collection of passages in the Old and New Testament. The list of passages used is in the back of the book. See if you can guess where a few of these sentences are found:

How can a young man keep his way pure? By keeping it according to Your Word. Your Word I have treasured in my heart, that I may not sin against You. Give me understanding, that I may observe Your law and keep it with all my heart. Make me walk in the path of Your commandments, for I delight in it: Your word is a lamp to my feet and a light to my path. I will never forget Your precepts, for by them You have revived me. I have inherited Your testimonies forever, for they are the joy of my heart. Those who love Your law have great peace, and nothing causes them to stumble. With all my heart I have sought You; do not let me wander from Your commandments. To whom shall we go? You have the words of eternal life. Your word is truth. The law of the LORD is perfect, restoring the soul; the testimony of the LORD is sure, making wise the simple. The precepts of the LORD are right, rejoicing the heart; the commandment of the LORD is pure, enlightening the eyes: They are more desirable than gold, yes, than much fine gold; sweeter also than honey and the drippings of the honeycomb: All Scripture is inspired by God, and profitable for teaching, for reproof, for correction, for training in righteousness; so that the man of God may be adequate, equipped for every good work:

Preach the word; be ready in season and out of season; reprove, rebuke, exhort, with great patience and instruction: For the word of God is living and active and sharper than any two-edged sword, and piercing as far as the division of soul and spirit, of both joints and marrow, and able to judge the thoughts and intentions of the heart: Therefore, putting aside all malice and all deceit and hypocrisy and envy and all slander, like newborn babes, long for the pure milk of the word, so that by it you may grow in respect to salvation, if you have tasted the kindness of the Lord: For the word of the cross is foolishness to those who are perishing, but to us who are being saved it is the power of God: Give attention to the public reading of Scripture, to exhortation and teaching. Receive the word implanted, which is able to save your souls. Be diligent to present yourself approved to God as a workman who does not need to be ashamed, accurately handling the word of truth.

But prove yourselves doers of the word, and not merely hearers who delude themselves. For if anyone is a hearer of the word and not a doer, he is like a man who looks at his natural face in a mirror; for once he has looked at himself and gone away, he has immediately forgotten what kind of person he was. But one who looks intently at the perfect law, the law of liberty, and abides by it, not having become a forgetful hearer but an effectual doer, this man will be blessed in what he does: Therefore, everyone who hears these words of Mine and acts on them may be compared to a wise man who built his house on the rock. And the rain fell, and the floods came, and the winds blew and slammed against that house; and yet it did not fall, for it had been founded on the rock. Everyone who hears these words of Mine and does not act on them will be like a foolish man who built his house on the sand. The rain fell, and the floods came, and the winds blew and slammed against that house; and it fell – and great was its fall: Heaven and earth will pass away, but My words will not pass away: The grass withers, and the flower falls off, but the Word of the LORD endures forever.

Man's Laws

People who don't trust God's laws put their trust in man's laws. Which one is better? God's laws never change and are preserved in His Word, the Bible; man's laws change with each election. God's laws are timeless; man's laws only exist for a certain time and a certain place. God's laws are beneficial for everyone; man's laws often favor the rich and powerful. God's laws are given for our spiritual benefit; man's laws having nothing to do with spirituality.

38

The Bible teaches that we should obey the laws of man in order to live peaceably on the earth (Romans 13:1-4). We shouldn't, however, put man's laws above God's laws. Our devotion should be to the God of the universe, not to the local or nationally elected official. Where man's laws and God's laws conflict, we must always do what God says. In Acts 4, Peter and John were arrested for preaching and healing in the name of Jesus. Before being released, they were told that they could no longer speak or teach about Jesus. But Peter and John knew they should not obey man's laws over God's laws. They said, "Whether it is right in the sight of God to give heed to you rather than to God, you be the judge; for we cannot stop speaking about what we have seen and heard" (Acts 4:19-20).

The Stain of Sin

You have sinned. Everyone in the world has sinned. If you say that you haven't sinned, you're a liar, and you make God a liar (1 John 1:8, 10). Unless you repent of your sins (Luke 13:3), confess Christ as Lord and Savior (Romans 10:10), are baptized into Christ (immersed in water) (Mark 16:16), and live faithfully until death (Revelation 2:10), you will die with your sins and be condemned for eternity. That is the plan of salvation for anyone who lived or lives after the Lord's church was established in Acts 2.

David often wrote about his sin (Psalm 51). He knew that sin stained his soul and separated him from God. Since he lived under the old law of Moses, he knew that the solution to his sin problem was obedience to that law. He struggled daily against his fleshly desires, but he knew that doing what God said was more important than giving into the temptations of Satan.

Time Out #3

Psalm 51 reminds us of the stain of sin when we break God's law. As this chapter admonishes us, we have the opportunity to respond to the gospel in the way God describes in the New Testament. Use a cup of clear water and food coloring to illustrate what sin does to our lives. Fill a clear cup with water until it's halfway full. Allow several students to use a dropper to place food coloring in the glass of water. Add several different colors, until the water is dark. Then pour one cup of bleach into the water, and watch as the stains go away and the water becomes clear. We can't do anything to remove the stains of sin, but God can.

Considering the effect of God's laws on his life, David ended Psalm 19 this way: "They [the laws] are more desirable than gold, yes, than much fine gold; Sweeter also than honey and the drippings of the honeycomb. Moreover, by them Your servant is warned; In keeping them there is great reward. Who can discern his errors? Acquit me of hidden faults. Also keep back Your servant from presumptuous sins; Let them not rule over me; Then I will be blameless, and I shall be acquitted of great transgression. Let the words of my mouth and the meditation of my heart be acceptable in Your sight, O LORD, my rock and my Redeemer" (vs. 10-14).

Things That Cannot Cure Sin

The Bible teaches us how to solve our sin problem, but many people refuse to follow that plan. Instead, they come up with all sorts of solutions that aren't really solutions at all—they're just ways that seem right in their own eyes.

Cure #1 - Excuses

The first two letters in "excuse" are the first two letters in "exit." An excuse is just an exit from responsibility. It's a way of saying, "I did it, but I shouldn't be punished for it." Some even use excuses to justify the sin, claiming that not only should they not be punished, but that the act itself isn't even a sin! Here are a few common excuses for certain sins:

1. "I stole those groceries, but I was really poor."
2. "The Bible says homosexuality is a sin (Romans 1:26-27; 1 Corinthians 6:9), but I can't help it because God made me this way. He just wants me to be happy."
3. "I know I hit him, but he made me mad."
4. "I despise rich people, but I'm not jealous. They should be more generous with their money."
5. "I'm not gossiping; I'm just sharing some news with other people."

Time Out #4

Take a few minutes and encourage everyone to "make some excuses." Try to come up with 5-7 excuses we are tempted to give for our sins. After you look at the list, ask the class how you should respond the next time those thoughts enter your mind.

Cure #2 - Good Intentions

Have you ever started a sentence with, "I meant to…" You did something wrong, and you try to justify it by focusing on what you intended to do. You would rather be judged for what you *didn't* do than by what you *did*. Someone once said, "The road to hell is paved with good intentions." In other words, good intentions do not save one's soul. God will not judge you based on what you meant to do. Second Corinthians 5:10: "For we must all appear before the judgment seat of Christ, so that each one may be recompensed for his deeds in the body, according to what he has done, whether good or bad."

Cure #3 - Good Works

This is the most socially acceptable alternative to solving one's sin problem. Someone says, "Look at all of the great things I've done in my life. I'm generous with my money. I'm nice to my neighbors. I attend worship services. I like doing what other people want to do instead of serving myself. Based on all of that, my sins should be forgiven."

Our good works cannot save us, however. On Judgment Day, many people will want God to see their good works and ignore their sins. But if we could save ourselves by doing enough good things, then why would Jesus need to come to earth and die for our sins? God could have said, "Just be a nice person, and you'll go to heaven." But we don't have a good works problem; we have a sin problem. And that problem can only be solved by obeying the gospel in the way that the Bible teaches.

Putting It All Together

1. This psalm focuses on God's design in creation. How do we see God's design in the world around us?
2. Alan Shepherd trusted that the laws of God never change. What are some laws of God in the world around us that we rely on every day (for instance, gravity)? What would happen if we couldn't rely on them?
3. Imagine being Peter and John when they were told not to teach about Jesus any more. What emotions would you feel in that situation?
4. Can you think of some things we mean to do but we never get around to doing? What keeps us from following up on our good intentions?
5. We cannot earn our salvation by doing good things. How do we receive salvation?

Taking It Home

This week, think of one way you can spend more time in God's Word. The book of Psalms has 150 psalms, and most months have 30 or 31 days. Try reading five psalms per day every day for a month. During that time, you will have read the entire book of Psalms.

Chapter 6

Doubting God's Presence

Psalm 22

Psalm Song Suggestion — "I Need Thee Every Hour"

Do you wish that Jesus were walking beside you every day of your life? I'm sure you do. Wouldn't life be awesome if He were sitting beside you right now or living in your house? No matter what happened to you, Jesus would be right there to support you. You could lean on His shoulder, ask Him for advice, or hold His hand. You might even want Jesus to call down fire from heaven and destroy all of the people who bothered you. (Some of Jesus's apostles actually asked Him to do that one time. See Luke 9:54).

Unfortunately, Jesus is no longer living among men. He ascended to heaven, and He is currently seated at the right hand of God. Because He isn't visible, you might think that Jesus no longer cares about you. You might feel like Jesus is unaware of your troubles. You pray and pray and pray, but it still doesn't *feel* like He's near you.

If it seems like Jesus is far away from you, then Psalm 22 addresses your concerns. It starts off depressing; the writer appears defeated. But by the end of the psalm, David, its author, reaffirms his faith in the abiding presence of God, and he is warmed by the love of His heavenly Father.

This isn't only a psalm that encourages those who doubt the Lord's presence, but it's also one that predicts many of the events that surrounded the last moments of Jesus' life. Jesus Himself quoted it while

Time Out #1

Take the "Fill in the Blank Challenge!" Listen to the beginning of several well-known phrases and see if you can fill in the rest of those quotes. Then, listen to the beginning of several Bible passages and see if you can fill in the rest of each of those verses.

He was suffering on the cross. Think about that! Do you quote Scripture while you're suffering? This psalm is so significant that Jesus quoted it even when blood poured from His body.

My God, My God, Why Have You Forsaken Me?

As we read the Bible, we assume that the inspired men who wrote the original texts inserted chapters and verses as they wrote. But they didn't. The Bible was divided into chapters and verses hundreds of years later. So how did people in Jesus' day tell the difference between one passage and another? Simple: They would often quote the first verse. For instance, if you said, "In the beginning God created the heavens and the earth," believers would know you were referencing Genesis 1, and they would know what that entire chapter was about, even if they couldn't quote the entire chapter.

The same is true with Psalm 22. When Jesus was in torment on the cross, He cried out, "My God, My God, why have You forsaken Me" (Matthew 27:46). Anyone who knew the Old Testament would have recognized that statement as Psalm 22:1. They would have understood that Jesus' thoughts were not on His tormenters, but on His Father in heaven. They knew He desperately wanted His suffering to end. However, they would have also known that Psalm 22 ends with great praise to God for His mercy: "For He has not despised nor abhorred the affliction of the afflicted; nor has He hidden His face from him; but when he cried to Him for help, He heard." (Psalm 22:24).

Even though Jesus' words seemed bitter and desperate, He knew that His Father in heaven would ultimately provide relief. Just a few days after being hanged on those wooden beams, Jesus ascended to heaven and left the pain and heartache of this world behind Him. Our Father in heaven always loved His only begotten Son.

Time Out #2

Print and distribute a version of Psalm 22 to each student. Read through the psalm together, and each time you come to a point in the psalm that has a parallel in Jesus' crucifixion, underline it on the page. Look up the passages that correspond to each underlined part of the psalm. Stop for a moment to reflect on how many of the psalms point to the coming Messiah.

Paul's Pain and Encouragement

The apostle Paul was arguably the most faithful Christian who ever lived … and possibly the most persecuted. In 2 Corinthians 11:23 he stated that he labored more and was imprisoned more than any other servant of Christ. He went on to state that he received 39 lashes from the Jews five separate times. (The Jews thought that 40 lashes would kill a man.) He was beaten with rods three times; he was shipwrecked three times; he was stoned; and he spent a day and night alone at sea (v. 25). Paul never knew the comfort of air-conditioned church buildings, paved interstate highways, nor a civil constitution that guaranteed him the freedom to practice his religion. But he remained committed to the Lord despite his discomforts and sufferings.

In his writings, Paul impressed on his readers that no matter how difficult life might be, God and His Son were always near. When he was preaching in Athens, Greece, he said that "(God) made from one man every nation of mankind to live on all the face of the earth, having determined their appointed times and the boundaries of their habitation, that they would seek God, if perhaps they might grope for Him and find Him, though He is not far from each one of us" (Acts 17:26-27). Paul essentially said that God made you, He knows where you live, and He is close to you every day.

In Romans 8, Paul listed the worst possible tragedies that a Roman Christian could face—famine, nakedness, murder, spiritual persecution—and then wrote, "But in all these things we overwhelmingly conquer through Him who loved us. For I am convinced that neither death, nor life, nor angels, nor principalities, nor things present, nor things to come, nor powers, nor height, nor depth, nor any other created thing, will be able to separate us from the love of God, which is in Christ Jesus our Lord" (Romans 8:37-39). No matter how tough life gets, God is right by your side, strengthening you with an unconditional love.

Just Because It Seems True Doesn't Mean It Is

If you think that the Boogy Man is in the closet at night, does that mean he is really in there? Of course not. If the boy in the history class thinks that the girl across the room likes him, does that mean she really likes him? Not necessarily. Our feelings don't always match the reality of a situation. That's why we should be careful not to assume things about God based solely on our emotions. The Bible should be our only guide when we have questions about the work of God.

Job's wife was one who made the tragic mistake of letting her emotions and circumstances affect her faith in God. As mentioned earlier, Job "was the greatest of all the men of the east" (Job 1:3). He owned thousands of sheep and camels and hundreds of oxen and donkeys. But God permitted Satan to destroy all of Job's possessions and children. Satan also afflicted Job with boils all over his body. All of this was allowed by God so that Satan would understand the extent of Job's unfailing faith. In a short span of time, Job went from Mr. Everything to Mr. Nothing. Figuratively speaking, He fell from the top of the mountain to the lowest valley. Remarkably, Job was able to maintain a good attitude shortly after those things took place. "Through all this Job did not sin nor did he blame God" (Job 1:22). His wife, however, let her emotions compromise her faith. She said to Job, "Do you still hold fast your integrity? Curse God and die!" (Job 2:9). Job's wife's first thought was to blame God for her problems. She assumed that God had abandoned her family. But she was mistaken.

God should never be blamed when we're hurting. James wrote: "Every good thing given and every perfect gift is from above, coming down from the Father of lights, with whom there is no variation or shifting shadow" (James 1:17). When we struggle with temptation, we might think that God is trying to get us to sin against Him—some sort of divine trick to find out if we actually prefer following Satan. James corrects that misunderstanding as well: "Let no one say when he is tempted, 'I am being tempted by God'; for God cannot be tempted by evil, and He Himself does not tempt anyone" (James 1:13). God is our Creator and the Source of all blessings—the Giver of grace, mercy, and forgiveness.

Endurance—The Underrated Virtue

You've probably heard of the phrase, "Take one for the team." It's a sports phrase that's usually applied to baseball players who have been hit by a pitch. It's a noble thing to take the pain of being hit so that you can reach first base and allow the next batter to drive you in with a hit. It's not fun to get hit by a pitch, but enduring that pain helps the player and the entire team succeed. Spiritually, endurance is a fundamental Christian virtue; we must endure the pains of life without losing our faith in God and His Son, so that we will receive our heavenly reward.

The word *endure* is defined as, "to suffer patiently." Paul and Job were two men in Scripture who suffered patiently. Their struggles are well-documented. Neither man enjoyed the pain he suffered. At times, both men questioned why they had to face so much turmoil. But because they suffered patiently and maintained their faith, God blessed them eternally. Notice how Jesus' half-brother, James, regarded Job: "We count those blessed who endured. You have heard of the endurance of Job and have seen the outcome of the Lord's dealings, that the Lord is full of compassion and is merciful. (James 5:11). Paul was aware of his difficulties *and* his blessings, and he proudly confessed both. "Therefore I am well content with weaknesses, with insults, with distresses, with persecutions, with difficulties, for Christ's sake; for when I am weak, then I am strong" (2 Cor. 12:10).

Time Out #3

Can you think of Christians you know who have endured difficult challenges and kept their faith? Take a few minutes to share examples with the class. What lessons can their lives teach us?

Common Teenage Trials

No two teenagers live the exact same lives. Some are raised in wealthy, two-parent homes; others are raised in poverty by one parent. But even though our experiences are different, there are a few trials that are common among most teenagers.

Rejection

All teenagers want to fit in. They want to sit at the "cool" table in the cafeteria and get picked to play for the good team. They also want the girl or guy of their dreams to fall in love with them. But life doesn't always work out that way. And when you hear the word *no*, it hurts. It's like getting punched in the stomach. When you feel the pain of rejection, remember that Jesus was rejected nearly every day of His life. About 700 years before Jesus was born, Isaiah prophesied that Jesus "was despised and forsaken of men, a man of sorrows and acquainted with grief" (Isaiah 53:3). He knows what you're going through. For every rejection, there will be twice as many people who will accept you for the person you are and appreciate your talents, friendship, and faithfulness.

Loss

Death is part of life. "You are just a vapor that appears for a little while and then vanishes away." (James 4:14). We don't want that to be true, but it is. The most faithful people on earth and the most godless people on earth will all eventually die. Losing a parent or grandparent at a young age can be particularly traumatic. The Bible teaches us that even though death is part of life, eternity is also part of life. We will spend eternity in heaven or hell. Since we know that death happens to all of us, shouldn't we take advantage of each day and live as faithfully as possible and show others how to be saved?

Temptation

"For all that is in the world, the lust of the flesh and the lust of the eyes and the boastful pride of life, is not from the Father, but is from the world" (1 John 2:16). Satan will tempt you every day to reject what God wants you to do. The devil wants you to cheat on tests at school, watch pornography, and curse while using God's name. It isn't a sin to be tempted—even Jesus was tempted. It is a sin, however, to submit to the temptation. Thankfully, you aren't helpless when you face temptation. If you remain faithful, God will give you the strength you need to do what's right. "No temptation has overtaken you but such as is common to man; and God is faithful, who will not allow you to be tempted beyond what you are able, but with the temptation will provide the way of escape also, so that you will be able to endure it" (1 Corinthians 10:13).

Time Out #4

Stop for a moment and make a list of some of the difficulties you face that haven't been mentioned. In one column, put the name of the challenge, and in the second column, write what you should pray for when facing that trial. Students might want to jot down a few points on that list and take that list home with them. It can help guide their prayers through the coming week.

Live and Learn

God promised us many things in the Bible, but He never promised that life would be easy. All of God's chosen patriarchs, prophets, and preachers—and even His only begotten Son—faced some degree of pain. And so will you. You will attend many funerals. You will get sick. Someone will break your heart. All we can do in the midst of these heartaches is remember that the Lord is still on the throne, and He promised that if we remain faithful to Him, we will live for eternity in the pain-free place called heaven.

"From You comes my praise in the great assembly;
I shall pay my vows before those who fear Him.
The afflicted will eat and be satisfied;
Those who seek Him will praise the LORD.
Let your heart live forever!"
(Psalm 22:25-26)

Putting It All Together

1. We began class by imagining what it would be like if Jesus were sitting next to you. If you could have a conversation with Jesus, what do you think He would tell you? Why?
2. Can you think of something a friend once told you, that he or she truly believed, that you later found out wasn't true?
3. How does it make you feel to know that Jesus experienced pain and temptations when He was on the earth?
4. Both Paul and Job showed tremendous patience when enduring suffering. Why is it so challenging to develop patience?
5. Psalm 22 ends with praise to God. Why does it end that way?

Taking It Home

Before class is over, think of one of the challenges you may face in the next week. Remember the passages about Job and Paul the next time you're in that situation. Next week, share with the class if that made a difference for you.

Chapter 7

God Gives You Everything You Need

Psalm 23

Psalm Song Suggestion — "Thank You, Lord!"

Newborn babies are great. They're so small, so innocent, and so loveable. They are also needy—*very* needy. They cannot feed themselves, change their diapers, or communicate with anyone around them. They are totally dependent on their parents. Even when those babies get much older, they still depend upon their parents for the basic necessities of life.

In Psalm 23, David expresses his dependence upon God. He knew that he was helpless without the blessings of his heavenly Father. Not only had God given David the necessities of life, but He also gave him an abundance of gifts that David didn't deserve. All Christians have been blessed by God in the same way. That's why Psalm 23 is the most recognized psalm in the world. It's read at nearly every funeral and is etched into grave markers and monuments throughout America. It's a love letter to God. You should memorize Psalm 23 (if you haven't already done so), and quote it to yourself and others for the rest of your life.

Time Out #1

As a class, take a few minutes to memorize Psalm 23. Repeat each phrase, until you can say it without looking at each verse. Put all the phrases together until you have the entire psalm memorized. It probably won't take as long as you think!

The Providence of God

Psalm 23 is poetic, like all the other psalms. David used vivid illustrations to show how much God had done for him. God gave David "green pastures" (v. 2) and "quiet waters" (v. 2). He led David down "paths of righteousness" (v. 3) and restored his soul (v. 3). David's cup overflowed (v. 5).

Notice that David didn't say that God had performed great miracles in his life. God, through His infinite wisdom and power, worked in David's life according to His will. The theological term for that process is *providence*. That word isn't used in the Bible; it's just a way to describe how God works in the lives of men today without miracles.

In the book of Genesis, we read about Joseph's life. He understood the providence of God. You may already know the story of how Joseph's brothers planned to kill him but decided to sell him into slavery instead. Joseph eventually ended up in Egypt, where his life had more twists and turns than a TV miniseries. But no matter what happened, God blessed Joseph. Genesis 39:2 states: "The LORD was with Joseph, so he became a successful man." Later, Potiphar, an officer who David worked for, threw Joseph into jail after Potiphar's wife falsely accused Joseph of rape. Yet again, "the LORD was with Joseph and extended kindness to him" (39:21).

Through a series of bizarre circumstances, Joseph was released from jail and gained high rank in the Egyptian government. Then a massive famine hit Egypt, just as Joseph had predicted (Genesis 41:30). Joseph's brothers traveled to Egypt to get food, and it was there that they met Joseph. Joseph had every right to be bitter, angry, and spiteful toward his brothers, but he wasn't. Instead, he acknowledged that God had been with him the entire way, and that if the brothers hadn't sold him into slavery, he wouldn't be in a position to help them through the famine. Joseph said to his brothers, "Now do not be grieved or angry with yourselves, because you sold me here, for God sent me before you to preserve life ... God sent me before you to preserve for you a remnant in the earth, and to keep you alive by a great deliverance" (Genesis 45:5,7).

Even though weak human beings make stupid decisions, God's will can still be accomplished. He can still use our foolishness to produce good in our lives. When we pray, we call on the Creator of the world to act for us. When He blesses us, we should express our thankfulness to

Time Out #2

Think about how Joseph felt when he was in a pit after being sold into slavery or when he was sitting in a jail cell after being falsely accused. Allow a few students to share how they would have felt in his position. What would have caused him to be able to forgive his brothers instead of holding a grudge?

Him through prayer and worship. David did that in Psalm 23. Augustine of Hippo, an early Christian theologian and philosopher, once said, "Trust the past to God's mercy, the present to God's love, and the future to God's providence."

What Does That Mean?

There are a few phrases in Psalm 23 that might be confusing to you. In verse one, David wrote, "The LORD is my shepherd, I shall not want." When I was a child, I understood the shepherd part, but I didn't understand "I shall not want." Does it mean that David did not want God? Of course not. He just meant that God supplied him with everything he needed. David didn't feel worried or anxious since God was his provider. "Every good thing given and every perfect gift is from above, coming down from the Father of lights, with whom there is no variation or shifting shadow" (James 1:17).

Another unusual phrase is in verse five: "You prepare a table before me in the presence of my enemies..." David isn't describing an actual table that God built. The table represented the vast array of food and water that God supplied for David. The abundance of those blessings was clearly seen by David's enemies. From the beginning of time, God has provided for his people. The Garden of Eden was filled with everything Adam and his wife needed. When the children of Israel were in the wilderness, they had daily manna to eat. Today, we're commanded to thank God for supplying our "daily bread" (Matthew 6:11). David's cup wasn't just full, it was running over. God blesses us in the same ways today.

Finally, David ends the famous psalm by stating, "Surely goodness and lovingkindness will follow me all the days of my life, and I will dwell in the house of the LORD forever" (v. 6). David surely lived in many houses throughout his life. He slept under the stars in the open field as a shepherd, and he slept in fine houses as the king of Israel. But he longed for a permanent dwelling in the "house of the LORD." Some believe that David was referring to the temple; others suggest that David was writing about heaven. Either way, David resolved to be in the presence of God forever. He wasn't satisfied anywhere else.

What Would Your 23rd Psalm Sound Like?

Have you ever put yourself into the Bible? Have you ever thought, *If I were there that day, what would I say and do?* It's an effective way to make the Bible come to life. In this case, if you were David, and you were about to write Psalm 23, what would you write? How would you express your love for God and His blessings? It will be easier to write your psalm if you consider these three themes.

Theme #1 - Count Your Blessings

Johnson Oatman, Jr. wrote the famous hymn *Count Your Blessings*. In the chorus we sing, "Count your blessings, name them one by one. Count your blessings, see what God hath done." When is the last time you counted the things God has done in your life? They would be too many to count, but you could try anyway. It's hard to complain to God about what you don't have if you're constantly reminding yourself of what God has given you.

President Abraham Lincoln was a man who experienced great achievements and incredible defeats. His mother died when he was 9. He lost several elections prior to becoming the President of the United States. Throughout his presidency, the country was at war. Only one of his four children (Robert) lived to adulthood; 12-year-old Willie Lincoln died while Lincoln was president, in 1862. But even in the midst of unimaginable sorrow, Lincoln said this in a speech in 1863: "We have been the recipients of the choicest bounties of heaven; we have been preserved these many years in peace and prosperity; we have grown in numbers, wealth and power as no other nation has ever grown. But we have forgotten God. We have forgotten the gracious hand which preserved us in peace and multiplied and enriched and strengthened us, and we have vainly imagined in the deceitfulness of our hearts, that all these blessings were produced by some superior wisdom and virtue of our own." That was Lincoln's way of counting his blessings.

Time Out #3

Take a few minutes to have a "blessings brainstorm." Divide the class into two groups, and see which group can be the first to write down 30 different blessings God has given them.

Theme #2 - The Greatest Pleasure Is Being With the Lord

God is everywhere. He knows what we do in secret (Matthew 6:4, 6). So, God is not in a place that has an address. The apostle Paul told the Athenians, "…in Him we live and move and exist…" (Acts 17:28). Being with the Lord is about devoting yourself to the things of God. David wanted to live in the house of the Lord forever because that meant he could leave all of the pain and frustration of this world.

It is interesting, however, that so many people want to be with the Lord forever in heaven, but only if they can take part of this world with them. They see heaven as a place that has endless amounts of their favorite things on earth. Athletes picture ball fields as far as the eye can see. Pet lovers imagine rolling hills where their pets can play without need of food or medicine. Chocoholics hope for rivers of endless chocolate so they can indulge their cravings. But none of those ideas are consistent with the biblical view of heaven, and David didn't think of material things when he thought of dwelling in the house of the Lord forever. He just wanted the enduring, soul-satisfying peace that is found with God, which is beyond comprehension (Philippians 4:7).

You can "be with God" every day. You can study His Word, the Bible. You can pray many times a day. You can identify people in your congregation or community who need assistance and do something—anything—to make their day a little bit brighter. When we grow in our faith, worship, and serve others, we're as close to God as we can be on earth. Hopefully others will see our commitment and be converted to Jesus Christ (Matthew 5:16).

Theme #3 - Life Is Easier When the Lord Is Your Guide

Notice all of the active verbs David uses to describe God's presence in his life. He states that God "makes" (v. 2), "leads" (v. 2), "restores" (v. 3), "guides" (v. 3), "prepares" (v. 5), and "anoints" (v. 5). That is why David called the Lord his shepherd—God did all the things for David that a common shepherd would do for his sheep. We would be like helpless sheep if we didn't have God as our guide. We wouldn't know how or why we were made, we would have no purpose, and we wouldn't know what happens after we die. Life would have no meaning without divine guidance.

Who is your guide? When you read verse one, put the emphasis on "The Lord." Those two words separate the Christian from non-believers. We believe that the Lord is our guide (shepherd), while the world chooses other people and things as their guides. The world is often guided by the love of money, illicit sexual behavior, and the pursuit of fame. We're guided by the light and love of God. We endeavor to follow His will.

Ages ago, Joshua was bold in proclaiming who was going to be his guide in life. Shortly before his death, Joshua encouraged the Israelites to follow God. He reminded them of all that the Lord had done for them in the past and then made his bold declaration: "If it is disagreeable in your sight to serve the LORD, choose for yourselves today whom you will serve: whether the gods which your fathers served which were beyond the River, or the gods of the Amorites in whose land you are living; but as for me and my house, we will serve the LORD" (Joshua 24:15).

Time Out #4

Have everyone take out a blank sheet of paper and write their own Psalm 23. Walk through each of the themes above, giving them time to write each section. Allow 2-3 to read theirs aloud. Have students take theirs home with them. Plan to read it at least three times during the week. Make sure you have everyone's cell number, and sometime on Monday, text them all the phrase "Count your blessings." That will be their cue to take a few minutes to count their blessings and read their psalm. Sometime on Wednesday, text them all the phrase, "The greatest pleasure is being with the Lord." That will be their signal to take a few minutes to re-read their psalm and say a silent prayer. Some time on Friday, text them all the phrase, "Life is easier when the Lord is your guide." This will be their reminder to re-read their psalm and then spend five extra minutes reading a psalm from Scripture that hasn't yet been covered in class.

It's Time to Trust

Psalm 23 teaches us a lot about God, but it also shows us David's dependence upon God. David trusted God. David didn't always do the right thing; he was a frail human being. But David knew that God was in control.

Do you trust God? That is the essence of faith. Do you trust Him to save your soul if you obey the gospel? Do you trust Him to allow you to live forever in heaven? Do you trust that the Bible is His communication with you? Are you willing to follow His commandments and live for Him? Psalm 23 is David telling God, "I trust you with my life."

Can you say the same thing?

Putting It All Together

1. Why do you think Psalm 23 is one of the most well-known passages in the Bible?
2. Think about the story of Joseph. How would you have felt when you were sitting in a pit, being sold into slavery, or holding onto the bars of a prison cell? What can you learn from Joseph that will help you through difficult times?

3. As human beings, we tend to forget about all the blessings God has given us. What can we do to change that?

4. What changes in our lives when we allow the Lord to guide us?

5. When is it hard for us to trust in God? Why is trust sometimes difficult?

Taking It Home

Take home your copy of your own Psalm 23, and read it three different times this week. Your teacher should text some reminders to you; see if your week goes differently when you remind yourself of God's blessings.

Chapter 8

Facing Your Enemies

Psalm 27
Psalm Song Suggestion – "The Battle Belongs To The Lord"

The word *phobia* is defined as "an extreme or irrational fear of or an aversion to something." The list of phobias is endless. There is triskaidekaphobia, which is the fear of the number 13. If you're afraid of heights, you have acrophobia. When I was a child, I hated going to the doctor, because I had trypanophobia—a fear of needles. And all of us to some degree have thanatophobia, a fear of death.

President Franklin D. Roosevelt was elected in 1932 at the beginning of the Great Depression. The stock market had crashed a few years earlier. The value of money was declining, and the unemployment rate was rising quickly. The American people were afraid. So, in his first inaugural address, President Roosevelt tried to ease their concerns and lift their spirits. Early in the speech, he said, "So, first of all, let me assert my firm belief that the only thing we have to fear is fear itself—nameless, unreasoning, unjustified terror which paralyzes needed efforts to convert retreat into advance."

But President Roosevelt wasn't the first person to recognize the paralyzing nature of fear. Centuries earlier, Jesus addressed worry in the Sermon

Time Out #1

Take a few minutes to share the list of fears found in the teacher's guide in the back of the book. Then have your class determine at least three fears that Christians face. They might talk about the fear of being rejected by friends for their beliefs, the fear of standing out because they do things differently, etc. Try to come up with creative, official sounding names, like "outcastaphobia" (fear of being an outcast).

on the Mount, which is a symptom of fear. He said we should not worry about the necessities of life (Matthew 6:25-32); the birds and the flowers do not worry about those things, and the Lord provides for them. He ended that theme by simply stating, "So do not worry about tomorrow; for tomorrow will care for itself. Each day has enough trouble of its own" (Matthew 6:34). That was the Lord's way of saying, "Don't be afraid. Take one day at a time."

Where David Found Courage

King David faced many scary things in his life. He faced a bear and a lion when he was young (1 Samuel 17:36). A few years later, he was confronted by Goliath, the greatest warrior in the Philistine army (I Sam. 17:41). When King Saul became overwhelmed by jealousy when David's popularity grew, he determined to kill David (1 Samuel 19:1). From his early years through adulthood, David's life was threatened . . . but he survived. He proudly proclaimed that he killed the lion and the bear. When the Israelite army was too afraid to face Goliath, David volunteered, and he killed the giant. Saul was never able to kill David, although he used many methods. So why was David so victorious in life? Where did he find confidence and strength?

Time Out #2

David was able to defeat enemies who were bigger than he was – a lion, a bear, and a giant. Divide the class into groups, and give each group the challenge of thinking of four examples where God gave a victory to someone or some group when it seemed unlikely. The first group that gets a list of four and hands it to the teacher wins.

In Psalm 27, David makes something perfectly clear: God has saved him from every fearful thing. "The LORD is my light and my salvation; whom shall I fear? The LORD is the defense of my life; whom shall I dread?" (v.1). He knew that he wasn't quick enough to escape a raging lion or bear. He knew that his own two arms were not strong enough to kill Goliath. King Saul was older and more experienced at warfare than David. But none of that mattered as long as God was fighting for him.

But even though God had blessed his life abundantly in the past, David knew he would face many more scary moments, so he pleaded for God's future protection. "Do not hide Your face from me, do not turn your servant away in anger; You have been my help; do not abandon me nor forsake me, O God of my salvation!" (v. 9). David didn't think that God would stop caring for him; God's love never changes (Romans 8:38-39). David is simply declaring that he will never leave God. He is showing his full faith in God's love and protection.

This psalm ends like many others—with an encouragement for the reader to believe and practice the things mentioned in the psalm: "Wait for the LORD; be strong and let your heart take courage; yes, wait for the LORD" (v. 14). Modern technology has trained us to think that any problem can be solved instantly, by clicking a computer mouse or a dialing 7 digits on a phone. But God doesn't often move that quickly. Even in the slower world in which David lived, he and others'needed to know that God's plan should be trusted above all else.

Who Are Your Enemies?

David had real, identifiable enemies throughout his life. All of his enemies could have killed him at any moment, but God spared him. So if a man who was described as "a man after God's own heart" (1 Samuel 13:14; Acts 13:22) had enemies, surely you have enemies as well. You might just have a few enemies, or you might have hundreds. Your enemies might be thoughts that live in your head, or they might be people who live in your neighborhood. No matter how many you have or where they are, you can face your enemies either with God or without Him. David would tell you to go with God. The Bible identifies several enemies Christians face.

Enemy #1 - Satan

The Hebrew word for Satan means "adversary," so Satan is the enemy to all God's people by definition. The apostle Peter explained Satan's activities by stating, "Be of sober spirit, be on the alert. Your adversary, the devil, prowls around like a roaring lion, seeking someone to devour" (1 Peter 5:8). Paul was also aware of Satan's operations, so he encouraged the Ephesians to be ready to fight him.

Put on the full armor of God,
so that you will be able to stand firm
against the schemes of the devil.
For our struggle is not against flesh and blood,
but against the rulers, against the powers,
against the world forces of this darkness,

against the spiritual forces of wickedness
in the heavenly places.
(Ephesians 6:11-12)

Paul stated that our struggle shouldn't be against men and women; our struggle is against the work of Satan. He is the one who is tempting and influencing men and women to do evil. The devil tempted Eve in the first sin (Genesis 3:1,6). He entered the heart of Judas (John 13:2). And he is tempting you every day to give in to your lusts (James 1:14).

Someone once said that the greatest trick the devil ever pulled was convincing the world that he didn't exist. That might be true. As soon as we think that Satan isn't real, we let down our guard and expose our hearts to evil. Satan has convinced our culture that having sex with your boyfriend or girlfriend is morally OK. He wants us to think that a little lie here or there is acceptable. Above all, he has persuaded many Christians to think that declaring something to be right or wrong is judgmental... and judgmentalism is the only *real* sin. But the Bible says that Satan is wrong. Sex is for marriage (Genesis 2:24); lying is a sin (Revelation 21:27); and we should all practice righteous judgment and declare right things right and bad things bad (1 Thessalonians 5:21-22).

Time Out #3

Satan is our enemy, and Scripture reminds us of that fact repeatedly. Think about the usual picture of Satan. What comes to mind? A tail? A pitchfork? A handlebar mustache? Now reread 1 Peter 5:8. How does Peter describe Satan? A roaring lion is dangerous. If we understand the power of Satan at work, we'll understand the importance of looking for temptations and avoiding them.

Enemy #2 - False Teachers

Satan is the ultimate enemy, but his influence is clearly seen in many areas of life. Often in the New Testament, Christians are commanded to oppose false teachers. They are enemies to the true gospel. Second Peter 2:1 states: "But false prophets also arose among the people, just as there will also be false teachers among you, who will secretly introduce destructive heresies, even denying the Master who bought them, bringing swift destruction upon themselves." When Paul was leaving the Ephesian elders in Acts 20, he warned them, "Be on guard for yourselves and for all the flock ... I know that after my departure savage wolves will come in among you, not sparing the flock; and from among your own selves men will arise, speaking perverse things, to draw away the disciples after them" (Acts 20:28-30).

Just because somebody wrote a popular book about Jesus, and just because somebody is preaching in front of a large audience, that doesn't necessarily mean that he or she is teaching the truth of Scripture. You have to be diligent in your study of the Bible to know that what you're reading or hearing is true. David said that knowing God's Word kept

Time-Out #4

Choose one student to be a "spiritual sketch artist." Have each member of the class call out characteristics of someone who is a genuine teacher from God, as opposed to a false teacher. The student will write those characteristics on the board (and can even draw a picture of a person next to it). Once you have several written on the board, look at those characteristics and ask, "What often keeps us from living like this?"

him from sinning (Psalm 119:11), and the Bereans made sure that what the apostles were teaching was accurate by examining the Scriptures daily (Acts 17:11).

The Secret Service is in charge of investigating people who produce counterfeit money. It would be impossible for them to find out all the possible ways a $100 bill could be faked. So, they make the process simpler. They become experts in *real* $100 bills, so they can easily identify a fake. We should do the same when it comes to matters of faith. If we know God's Word, we can easily recognize a false teacher.

Worldliness

James, the half-brother of Jesus, made this shocking statement: "You adulteresses, do you not know that friendship with the world is hostility toward God? Therefore whoever wishes to be a friend of the world makes himself an enemy of God" (James 4:4). Wow! I would hate to be an enemy of God because all of God's enemies lose! James says that if you become a friend of the world, you're on the wrong side of God. He also says that you are an "adulteress." What does he mean?

The word *world* in this verse means things in this life that are contrary to God's will. The majority of the people in the world and a majority of the things done in the world aren't godly—they are sinful to the core. Therefore, the world is our enemy. We have to live in it, but we don't have to live by its standards. Paul wrote: "And do not be conformed to this world, but be transformed by the renewing of your mind, so that you may prove what the will of God is, that which is good and acceptable and perfect" (Romans 12:2).

James described those who love the world as "adulteresses." He's making an analogy to marriage. If a woman is devoted to her husband, she will not have sex with another man. As Christians, we should be devoted to God. We shouldn't betray Him by showing devotion to the world. If we devote ourselves to worldly things, we become spiritual cheaters or "adulteresses."

You Can Defeat Your Enemies

No one goes through life undefeated. We all fail. David failed often. His most outrageous sin was when he lusted for Bathsheba, committed adultery with her, covered up the sin, and then sent her husband to the front of the battle to be killed, which eventually happened. He broke four of the Ten Commandments in just one chapter, 1 Samuel 11. Even though your sins might not be that shocking, you have sinned nonetheless (Romans 3:23). And even though your enemies might not be lions and bears and giants (Oh my!), your enemies still have the power to destroy your family, your church, and ultimately, your soul.

However, you can have victory when you put your faith in God and His Son, Jesus Christ of Nazareth. The same God who led the Israelites out of a 400-year Egyptian bondage is on your side. When you do His will by following His commandments, He will bless your life.

None of your enemies are stronger than God.

Putting It All Together

1. What does David's life teach us about overcoming fear?
2. How does it make you feel to realize that God's love never changes?
3. When we realize the power of Satan and temptations in our lives, how does that change our perspective on life?
4. Think of a person you have known was a sincere, dedicated Christian, living for God every day. What did that person do to make his faith known to others?
5. Why is it so easy to allow the world to influence more than our faith in God? What can we do about it?

Taking It Home

Read the first verse of Psalm 27, and remember that if the Lord is your light, you don't have to fear anyone. This week, when something happens at school or at home that brings up fear about what other people will think or what your friends might say, repeat this verse to yourself: "The Lord is my light and my salvation; whom shall I fear?"

Chapter 9

The Power of God

Psalm 46

Psalm Song Suggestion – "Be Still and Know"

Tim Keller describes an illustration that a Sunday School teacher gave in 1970 that changed his life. She said, "Let's assume that the distance between the earth and the sun (93 million miles) was reduced to the thickness of this sheet of paper. If that is the case, then the distance between the earth and the nearest star would be a stack of papers 70 feet high. And the diameter of the galaxy would be 310 miles high. The galaxy is just a speck of dust in the universe, yet God holds the universe together by the word of His power."

The teacher then looked at her students and asked, "Now, is this the kind of person you ask into your life to be your assistant?" The answer to that question is obvious: No! You pray that God will be *in charge* of your life because He is so powerful. (From the sermon *The Gospel and Your Self.*)

Until the world accepts and appreciates the power of God, they will never be converted. In Romans 1, Paul states that the world can see the power of God by just observing the world around them. "For since the creation of the world His invisible attributes, His eternal power and divine nature, have been clearly seen, being understood through what has been made, so that they are without excuse." (Romans 1:20). In other words, at judgment day, the world will not be able to say, "I wasn't smart enough to understand You," or, "I couldn't know You because nobody ever told me about You." The reality of God is seen by every person every day in the beauty of His creation.

Psalm 46 is designed to help us recognize and praise the power of God. The notation above this psalm states that it was a song written by (or possibly for) the sons of Korah, and it is set to Alamoth. Scholars are unsure of the specific meaning of Alamoth, and they don't know what Selah means at the end of verses 3, 7 and 11. Some think that Alamoth might be soprano singers, and Selah might just represent a pause in the song, but no one can know for sure. Those are obscure Hebrew words.

Circumstances Change, God Doesn't

A Frenchman named Francois de la Rochefoucauld once said, "The only thing constant in life is change." We might *want* things to stay exactly as they are, but we know they won't. We are healthy for a while, and then we get sick. We get hired for a job, and then we quit or get fired. Flowers bloom in the spring, and then they die in the fall. Ecclesiastes teaches us that there is a time for everything on earth, and that God has made everything appropriate in its time (Ecclesiastes 3:11). We cannot slow down time, and we cannot dictate the future. Life is always changing. Jesus said, "So do not worry about tomorrow; for tomorrow will care for itself. Each day has enough trouble of its own" (Matthew 6:34).

Time Out #1

Think back to this time last year. What has changed in the past year? Maybe you're at a different school with different teachers, or maybe you've even moved to a different house during that time. Make a list of all the changes you can think of in the past twelve months.

Psalm 46 begins by reassuring the reader that God gives us peace when everything around us seems out of control:

> *God is our refuge and strength,*
> *A very present help in trouble.*
> *Therefore we will not fear,*
> *though the earth should change*
> *And though the mountains slip*
> *into the heart of the sea;*
> *Though its waters roar and foam,*
> *Though the mountains quake at its swelling pride* (vs. 1-3).

Your circumstances will change dramatically from ages 18 to 25. Your faith and standard of morality will be challenged. You will likely move out of your house after high school graduation or college graduation, which will require you to get a job, shop for your own clothes and food, pay for your own car, gasoline, and insurance, find a place to buy or rent, and survive in a world that is heavily influenced by Satan. You might also need to find another congregation if you move far enough away from your current home. Your world will look entirely different from the one in which you grew up.

Are you ready for that change? God doesn't care where you live, what car you drive, or what your salary is. He doesn't care if you rent an apartment or buy a house. He is only concerned about your faith. Will you remain faithful to Him when your circumstances change? Will He be your refuge and strength? The Bible teaches us that faith isn't a one-time event or just something we have when life is easy. Your last day on earth should be the most faithful day of your life, no matter what your circumstances are. "And without faith it is impossible to please Him, for he who comes to God must believe that He is and that He is a rewarder of those who seek Him" (Hebrews 11:6). "Be faithful until death, and I will give you the crown of life" (Revelation 2:10). "I have fought the good fight, I have finished the course, I have kept the faith" (2 Timothy 4:7). "…[L]et us also lay aside every encumbrance and the sin which so easily entangles us, and let us run with endurance the race that is set before us" (Heb. 12:1).

Remember What God Did In The Past

One of the greatest blessings God ever gave us is the gift of memory. We cannot predict the future, but God allows us to see things from our past, which helps us learn lessons and cherish the moments we had with loved ones who are gone. It also helps us praise God for His past kindnesses. Twice in Psalm 46 we read, "The God of Jacob is our stronghold" (vs. 7, 11). The psalmist knows that the same God who led His people out of Egypt, parted the Red Sea, guided the Israelites through the desert and eventually into the Promised Land, cares for him with the same unconditional love.

God has a perfect résumé. God created the world, and then He made man in His image, with an eternal soul. Even after man sinned, God told him that One is coming who would solve that sin problem forever by crushing the head of Satan (Genesis 3:15). He not only has blessed those who obey Him, but He has also blessed sinners by giving them food, clothing, and shelter. When we consider what God has done, we should be willing to do anything and go anywhere in His name.

Since we can remember the great blessings of God from the past, why wouldn't we trust His promises for the future? One of the most comforting and reassuring verses in the Bible is Romans 8:28: "And we know that God causes all things to work together for good to those who love God, to those who are called according to His purpose." He caused Joseph's adventurous life to work together for good by putting him in a position where he could feed his family during the famine. Even though Abraham had to go through the gut-wrenching task of strapping his son to an altar to kill him, God caused him to be stopped, and his son Isaac was spared. As a Christian, Paul was arrested, beaten, imprisoned, and shipwrecked, but God used all of those tragedies to produce good things in Paul's life. Even if we cannot see an immediate good, God has promised those who obey Him that they will receive eternal good in a place called heaven.

Let God Be God

Verse 10 of Psalm 46 seems strange at first. The New American Standard Bible translates the verse as, "Cease striving and know that I am God; I will be exalted among the nations, I

Time Out #2

Bill McDonald of Centerville, Tennessee was conducting a youth devotional at his house. He wanted to teach the young people to trust God, so he set his 2-year-old child on the mantel of his fireplace. He then asked for a volunteer to come forward. He said, "Hold out your hands, and say, 'Jump!'" The teenager did as he was told, but the child didn't move. Another teenager also failed to get the child to jump off the mantel. After the teenagers sat down, Bill turned around to his child and said, "Jump!" and the child leaped into his arms. Why did the child jump into his arms and not into the arms of the teenagers? Children trust their daddies; the child didn't trust the teenagers. Bill always caught his children when they jumped.

God will always catch us when He says, "Jump!" We can trust him because of all the times He caught others when they were falling. We can be faithful to Him because He has always been faithful to us.

will be exalted in the earth." The first half of the verse is familiar to many Christians, and they know it by the King James Version: "Be still, and know that I am God…" The New American Standard expresses the literal meaning.

Time Out #3

As a class, pause and be silent for two full minutes. This will feel like longer than it really is. After the two minutes have ended, share how that made you feel. Why is silence so difficult for us?

If you tell someone today to be still, that person will just stop moving his/her body. But the meaning here has nothing to do with physical motion; God wants us to stop thinking that we can control everything. The original Hebrew word here could also be translated "let go" or "relax."

There Is a God, and You Are Not Him

God made a similar statement to the Israelites through Isaiah the prophet: "For My thoughts are not your thoughts, nor are your ways My ways" (Isaiah 55:8). You only have to read a small section of the Bible in order to understand this simple fact: You are not God. You can only know so much, think so much, run so far, and live so long. You're limited. Nineteenth-century German philosopher, Friedrich Nietzsche, has been credited with saying, "There cannot be a God because if there were one, I could not believe that I was not he." Many people believe the same thing but probably have never said it that way. But the Bible makes it clear in this psalm and in other areas: There is a God, and you are not Him.

Our 21st century American culture demands that we care about *everything*—the environment, government, every story that someone links on Facebook and Twitter, education, gas prices, constitutional rights, etc. We're constantly told that in order to fix all of those issues, we have to get involved and do something. If we could all just band together—the world tells us—we could ultimately solve every problem we face.

That's a lie.

As long as sinful, weak, mortal human beings are living on this planet, there will be problems that cannot be solved with human effort. If we could solve these problems, we wouldn't need God or His Son Jesus. God would have just said, "Figure it out on your own. You don't need Me." When the Israelites approached Jericho, they saw a fortified city. God told them to march around that city once a day for six days and then seven times on the seventh day. The Israelites were obedient, and the walls fell down. Did the vibrations from their feet stomping on the ground cause the walls to collapse? Of course not. It was their obedience to God's plan that caused the walls to fall. Those Israelites would have been defeated if God had not fought for them.

Two verses of Scripture highlight our need to be obedient to God's plans. James wrote, "Humble yourselves in the presence of the Lord, and He will exalt you" (James 4:10). Also, Paul stated, "Be anxious for nothing, but in everything by prayer and supplication with thanksgiving let your requests be made known to God. And the peace of God, which surpasses all comprehension, will guard your hearts and your minds in Christ Jesus" (Philippians 4:6-7). In each verse, we're told that God will work for us when we humbly serve Him. That makes life a lot easier. It's always good to stop striving and know that God is God.

Sing About It

As I noted at the beginning of the chapter, this psalm was originally a song, as many psalms were. We don't know the tune of the song, we just know the lyric. It would be nice to know what this psalm sounded like when it was sung for the first time. First-century Christians sang these psalms frequently. In two different letters, Paul commanded that we teach, admonish (caution), and encourage one another with "psalms, hymns, and spiritual songs" (Ephesians 5:19; Colossians 3:16).

Think of all the songs you know by heart. Did you try to memorize those lyrics? Probably not. When a melody is attached to a lyric, the song becomes easy to remember. It's no wonder then that God, through His infinite wisdom, wanted us to sing praise to Him. Songs penetrate our hearts and minds in ways that spoken words cannot. They can be learned and recalled easily.

Psalm 46 was known and loved as a song by many children of God in the ancient world. It gave them encouragement. It reminded them that even though life is unpredictable, God is constant. He will lift us up when the world tries to push us down. He will tirelessly work on our

Time Out #4

Divide into groups for a "translating" session. You won't be translating the psalm into another language, but you will be translating the principles of this psalm into your everyday life. Encourage the students to look at the various phrases and restate them in their own words. Once you're done, have each group read its psalm out loud.

behalf when we're mentally and physically exhausted. He's stronger than anything we can comprehend, yet His arms are soft enough to receive the most damaged sinner. He truly is our refuge and strength.

Putting It All Together

1. According to Romans 1, how does God make Himself known to the world?

2. In Matthew 6:34, Jesus warns us not to worry about tomorrow. What are some reasons we usually worry about the future?

3. This psalm reminds us of the importance of trusting God. What are some reasons we know we can trust Him?

4. How does it make you feel to realize that there are some problems only God can solve but human beings cannot?

5. One of the reasons we worship through song is to teach spiritual truths. What is a song that is special to you that has taught you something?

Taking It Home

Choose a time this week where you "disconnect" from everything—your phone, computer, tablet, social media, etc. for at least 20 minutes. During that time, read Psalm 46, along with other passages of Scripture. Pray that you'll be able to regularly shut out all of life's distractions and remember that God is in control.

Chapter 10

Forgiveness and Renewal

Psalm 51

Psalm Song Suggestion – "Create in Me a Clean Heart"

David is one of the best known individuals in the entire Bible. If I asked you for his scriptural description, you might reply, "a man after God's own heart." That is probably the most famous phrase in all Scripture describing David. There is another phrase, though, that reveals something important about David's life. First Kings 15:5 states, "David did what was right in the sight of the LORD, and had not turned aside from anything that He commanded him all the days of his life, except in the case of Uriah the Hittite." This description is not quite as positive. It reminds us of what is probably the darkest chapter in David's life, but walking through that darkness can help us appreciate Psalm 51 and the forgiveness of God.

Second Samuel 11 gives us a storyline that would be plastered all over the Internet if it came out today. David, the king, is involved in an affair, and he uses his power to keep it a secret. This powerful king had decided to stay home while other kings were in battle. While he was walking on his roof one night, he caught sight of a woman bathing. That may sound strange to us, but bathing on the roof wasn't uncommon then. David didn't just glance at her, he kept looking. One of his servants told David who she was: Bathsheba, Uriah's wife. Uriah was one of David's mighty men who had faithfully fought for David in the past, but that didn't stop David from sending for her and committing adultery.

David might have thought it was all over, but after a little while, Bathsheba sent word to David that she was pregnant. Then, David had a decision to make. He called Uriah, his faithful soldier, back home, and he tried to set up a scenario where Uriah could go back home and see Bathsheba. This way, Uriah would assume that the child was his. Yet Uriah was too loyal to his

76

fellow soldiers to do that. David then sent Uriah into battle, telling his commander, Joab, to back away in battle so that Uriah would be killed. Once that happened, David took Bathsheba as his wife.

Wow! These events sound like they could come straight out of a movie, and if they did, David wouldn't be the good guy. We cheer for David when he fights Goliath, but we can't cheer for him in this story. Yet if we read Psalm 51, we get insight into David's heart, as he struggled with regret for the hurt his sin had caused.

Time Out #1

Think of some of the most famous people we read about in the Bible. Write down the names of the first five famous individuals that you can name. Can you think of sins they committed? List any mistakes they made that come to mind. Like David, every human follower of God is imperfect. God includes these examples so that we can see how imperfect followers can be used by a perfect God.

We might not cheer for him, but when we realize he was a sinner, we can identify with him.

Who Could It Hurt?

One of Satan's strategies for temptation is moving our focus away from the consequences of sin. He wants us to be so focused on how good it will feel that we don't think about how much it will hurt. Yet we know that sin has consequences, and David's example reminds us of that important fact.

When I was growing up, I learned a definition for the word *joy* that I still remember. One of my teachers told me to remember that each letter stood for a different word: "J" stood for *Jesus*, "O" stood for *Others*, and "Y" stood for *You*. You may have learned the same memory device. My teacher's point was that if we want to have joy, we need to put Jesus first in our lives, make concern for others our next priority, and focus on ourselves last. In fact, when Jesus was asked what the greatest command was in Matthew 22, He responds in verse 37 with these words: "You shall love the LORD your God with all your heart,

Time Out #2

Take a copy of Psalm 51, and underline every reference to sin. Read through it again, and circle every description of forgiveness (such as "purge me," "wash me," etc.). You can almost feel the passionate plea for forgiveness coming from the heart of David.

and with all your soul, and with all your mind." In verse 39, He follows that command up with this one: "You shall love your neighbor as yourself." Jesus reflected that same order when it comes to following Him; we need to put God first, others second, and ourselves last. This order is also evident when we think of how sin affects our life. As David's story reminds us, sin stands in the way of our relationship with God, it hurts others, and it affects ourselves.

Sin Hurts Our Relationship With God

In Psalm 51:4, David says something interesting. He tells God that his sin was against God and only God. That doesn't seem to make much sense does it? After all, Uriah is dead and Bathsheba has been taken from the life she knew and moved into David's palace. Yet, David tells God that his sin is only against God. He sounds like Joseph, back when he was a slave in Genesis 39. Joseph was doing well in the house of Potiphar, and he had achieved a high level of respect. Potiphar's wife seemed to notice that as well, and she made repeated attempts to convince Joseph to sleep with her (verse 10 tells us it happened day after day). When Joseph explains himself to her in verse 9, he says "How then could I do this great evil and sin against God?" He didn't mention the possibility of getting caught by his master or his guilty conscience. He pointed to God.

The most well-known parable Jesus ever told is probably the parable of the Prodigal Son in Luke 15. Take a few minutes to scan Luke 15:11-32 and remind yourself of that story. After the younger son has taken his inheritance and spent it all on things he shouldn't have, he comes to his senses. He starts thinking about what he should do, and he comes up with the plan of returning home. Notice what he plans to say to his father in verses 18-19: "I will get up and go to my father, and will say to him, 'Father, I have sinned against heaven, and in your sight; I am no longer worthy to be called your son; make me as one of your hired men." Just a few verses later, when he has come home and his father runs out to meet him, the prodigal son only manages to get through the first half of that statement. He informs his father that he has sinned against heaven and in his sight. Even in a parable, we see evidence that a sin affects our relationship with God above all else. This doesn't mean we shouldn't care about the way our sin affects others, but it does remind us that the ultimate problem with sin is that it creates separation in our relationship with God.

Sin Hurts Others

We usually think about how sin affects us, but what about the way it affects others? A few years ago, I heard a sermon title that stuck with me: "What is your sin going to cost me?" The question reminds us of the fact that our sins affect other people. According to the prophet Nathan in 2 Samuel 12, there were specific consequences in David's life. The sword would never depart from his house (meaning that violence and death would always plague his family—v. 10), one of his children would rise up against him (which Absalom did), a companion would sleep with his wives (which Absalom did), and the child conceived with Bathsheba would die. In the same chapter, we see the last prophecy fulfilled, as his child became sick and died. The next few chapters tell us about Amnon, who raped his half-sister Tamar, and her brother, Absalom, who avenged Tamar by murdering Amnon. Absalom would later overthrow his father David and eventually die in battle. Nathan's prophecies were true—violence did not leave David's household. These were lasting consequences to David's actions that affected many people.

Time Out #3

Take a few minutes as a class, and think about the unintended consequences of sin. Write a sin on the board, and then think of as many possible consequences of that sin as possible. The better we understand the impact our sins have on those we care about, the better we will be able to resist temptation.

Do we think about the way our sins affect other people? When we gossip about someone else or laugh at a rumor that isn't true, do we ever stop to think about how it makes them feel? Do we think about the different challenges they will face because of what other people are saying? When someone gives us the chance to cheat on a test, do we stop and think about what kind of example we're setting? What if there's someone who sees what we're doing and decides honesty isn't a big deal? Our example could encourage other people to accept behavior that isn't right. We need to ask this question: What will my sins cost other people?

Sin Hurts Us

Psalm 32 is another psalm that gives us insight into how David felt after he sinned. In verses 3 and 4, he writes, "When I kept silent about my sin, my body wasted away through my groaning all day long. For day and night Your hand was heavy upon me; my vitality was drained away as with the fever heat of summer." Can you hear the pain in that description? Right after Uriah was killed in battle and Bathsheba became David's wife, it might have seemed like David got away with it. On the outside, he might have seemed like the same old king, but he was in pain on the inside. The guilt he felt made life miserable. Has that ever happened to you? Have you ever done something wrong, and even though no one else knew about it, the guilt weighted you down?

We see how seriously David takes his sin in Psalm 51. In Psalm 51:5, he states that he felt like he had been sinning from the time he was born. The phrasing of this verse has caused a lot of discussion in the religious world. Some read, "Behold, I was brought forth in iniquity, and in sin my mother conceived me," and walk away claiming that David was born in sin. This verse is often used to support the thought that human beings are sinful from the time they're born, a teaching usually referred to as "original sin." Some might use this passage to claim that infants should be baptized, even though they don't understand right from wrong and cannot make the conscious decision to obey God. That idea simply isn't consistent with Scripture. In the New Testament, the only people who are baptized are those who are old enough to understand that they have sinned, believe in Jesus, turn their lives around, and willingly put Christ on in baptism.

Time Out #4

Stop and think about an area of your life in which you need to take responsibility. You don't have to share it with anyone other than God. Have a time of silent prayer where each class member can pray for God to provide strength and encouragement to take responsibility for this change.

Remember what we've learned about the psalms so far—they use figurative language to make a point. David isn't trying to support the idea of original sin; he is simply saying that this sin is weighing so heavily on him that he feels like he has always sinned. Have you ever made a mistake and been tempted to say to yourself, "I've always been like that"? That is how David felt, like he had always been a sinner.

Notice that he requests repeatedly that God would "wash him," "cleanse him," "and "purify him," etc. This is different than some of the psalms that ask God to act in their circumstances (defeat my enemies, etc.). This psalm doesn't ask God to change his circumstance but to change the psalmist. Do we ever need to take that approach—to ask for ourselves to be changed rather than our surroundings? It's easier to blame our situation or someone else than to take responsibility for ourselves.

Forgiveness Begins With God

David's plea to God in Psalm 51:10 is for a clean heart and a right spirit. He wants to be cleansed of his sins, and he realizes that can only happen through God. David was a powerful man, but there was nothing he could do to relieve himself of the guilt of his sin. All of his wealth couldn't buy it, and none of his advisors could give it to him. In 51:11-12, he pleads with God: "Do not cast me away from Your presence and do not take Your Holy Spirit from me. Restore to me the joy of your salvation, and sustain me with a willing spirit." In Psalm 32:5, David tells us about his appeal to God for forgiveness, writing, "I acknowledged my sin to you, and my iniquity I did not hide; I said, 'I will confess my transgressions to the LORD,' and You forgave the guilt of my sin."

If we're weighed down with guilt, forgiveness is found only in God. We might be able to find something that can numb our pain or momentarily distract us from our sins, but the ultimate solution to our sin can only be provided by God. He is faithful to His promises, and we can trust Him. In 1 John 1:9, the process is described this way, "If we confess our sins, He is faithful and righteous to forgive us our sins and cleanse us from all unrighteousness."

Putting It All Together

1. David was a man of great faith, yet he struggled with sin. What does that teach us?
2. In the parable of the Prodigal Son, the father is eagerly waiting to forgive him. Do we have the same reaction when people hurt us? Why or why not?
3. David's family had some serious issues. Even those who serve God may struggle with family issues. Why do you think God would include details about the struggles of His servants in the Bible?
4. When we are weighed down with guilt, forgiveness can only come from God. Yet we often turn to other things to distract us from our guilt or help us feel better momentarily. What are some examples of things we do to take our mind off our guilt?
5. How does it make you feel to know that God is faithful to forgive us?

Bringing It Home

Take time each day this week to read Psalm 51 and pray that area of your life where you need to take responsibility and live differently. Ask God to help you make the changes you need to make.

Chapter 11

The Compassion of the Eternal God

Psalm 103
Psalm Song Suggestion – "The Steadfast Love of the Lord"

Time Out #1

Imagine this: Someone hands you $100 and says, "You cannot keep this money. You have to give it all away within the next 24 hours. I don't care who gets it. Just be sure it's gone in a day." Would you go to the bank and get 100 $1 bills and give $1 to 100 people? Would you hand the entire $100 to one person? It would be a fun thing to do, but it would also be difficult to decide who would get that free money. Take a few minutes to decide what you would do with it and share it with the class.

Who Is My Neighbor?

If you're like most people, you would distribute the money in this order: family first, then friends, then strangers. We want to take care of the people who know us, look like us, act like us, and care about us. We feel like they deserve it, and we know that they'll use it wisely. We'll give whatever is left over to friends or needy strangers.

That was the thinking of ancient Israelites as well. By the time Jesus came into the world, they had developed an us-against-the-world type of thinking. When they learned the commandment to "love your neighbor as yourself" (Leviticis 19:18), they thought about Israelites first and foremost. An expert in the law of Moses once asked Jesus what he needed to do to inherit eternal life. Jesus asked him what the law told him to do, and the expert instantly quoted Deuteronomy 6:5 and Leviticus 19:18, the passages about loving God and loving your neighbor as yourself. Jesus told him he was correct, and that he should do those things. Then the expert got cocky and asked, "Who is my neighbor?" (Luke 10:29). The expert wanted Jesus to say that "neighbors" were only the Israelites, so that the expert could feel good about himself.

But instead, Jesus went on to tell the familiar parable of the Good Samaritan, about how a man who was beaten, left for dead, and ignored by a priest and Levite was finally helped by a Samaritan. Jesus then asked the expert, "Which of these three do you think proved to be a neighbor to the man who fell into the robbers' hands?" And he said, "The one who showed mercy toward him." Then Jesus said to him, "Go and do the same" (Luke 10:36-37).

Everyone on earth is your neighbor—your family, your friends, even strangers who might need special assistance. Psalm 103 describes the eternal compassion of God. It teaches us how God has every right to mistreat us because of our sins, but He doesn't. It teaches us how He defends the defenseless and pardons our sins. And He does all of it from His eternal throne in heaven.

Compassion

Have you ever had a gut feeling about something? Do you feel a knot in your stomach when you hear about a family whose house burned or a soldier who has been killed overseas? The Hebrew word that is translated "compassion" in the Old Testament is actually related to the womb or stomach. Even in the New Testament, when Jesus said that the Samaritan had compassion on the beaten man, He was essentially saying that the Samaritan was acting on a gut feeling. James stated that when we have that feeling, we need to act: "Therefore, to one who knows the right thing to do and does not do it, to him it is sin" (James 4:17). The one who acts on his gut feeling, however, will be blessed.

The compassion of God is more than just His gut feeling. His compassion is based on His perfect will for our lives. It's based on His eternal perspective on life. David wrote in Psalm 103: "Just as a father has compassion on his children, so the LORD has compassion on those who fear Him. For He Himself knows our frame; He is mindful that we are but dust" (vs. 13-14). The God who made the world with just His words could crush each of us with just a whisper; but He doesn't, because He knows we're frail. He knows we're not as majestic as Him. Even though we might deserve instant destruction as punishment for our sins, He shows His compassion by providing a way for us to be saved.

Jesus was the physical demonstration of God's compassion. He gave up the comforts of heaven to live in the dangerous world of man (Philippians 2:5-8). The Hebrew writer explained it this way: "For we do not have a high priest who cannot sympathize with our weaknesses, but One who has been tempted in all things as we are, yet without sin. Therefore let us draw near with confidence to the throne of grace, so that we may receive mercy and find grace to help in time of need" (Hebrews 4:15-16). The high priests in Israel were disconnected from the people in the clothes they wore, the ceremonial things they did in the temple, and the way they lived their lives in general. But Jesus isn't that kind of high priest for us. He understands our lives. He was tempted. Therefore, He showed compassion for man.

Since God and His Son show the ultimate compassion for us, we should go to them with confidence. You should never think about God and say, "He doesn't get it. He doesn't understand." Our advocate with the Father, Jesus Christ the righteous, knows exactly how we feel (1 John 2:1).

"The Lord is compassionate and gracious, slow to anger and abounding in lovingkindness" (Psalm 103:8).

Forgiveness

Psalm 103 also describes the extent of God's forgiveness. Since the book of Psalms is poetic, it's is easy for us to read certain phrases as symbolic and other phrases as literal, when the opposite might be accurate. For instance, verse 12 states: "As far as east is from the west, so far has He removed our transgressions from us." We might quickly read "As far as the east is from the west…" and just think that David is using some flowery poetry to make his point. But David is being literal. Think about it: If you started traveling north, you

Time Out #2

How does it make you feel to know that Jesus was tempted in every way as we are? Though our world might be different today, the temptations that are common to everyone remain the same. Think about it like a piano. Every piano has the same keys. It would be impossible to count how many different songs have been composed on a piano over the years. Picture a talented piano player; he might not have played every song ever composed, but he has played all the notes on all the keys. Jesus might not have faced the exact same situations that we have, but He has played "all the notes." We can know when we pray that Jesus understands us.

would eventually cross over the North Pole, and then you would be heading south. If you traveled east, would you ever start going west? Nope. East is always east, and west is always west. So, read that verse again: "As far as the east is from the west, so far has He removed our transgressions from us."

We sin when we miss the mark that God set for us, and every person on earth has sinned (Romans 3:23). All sins deserve punishment (Romans 6:23). That punishment was inflicted on animals under the old law, as the children of Israel were being reminded of their sins every time they made a sacrifice. Those sins were being pushed forward with each sacrifice, eventually ending up at the foot of the cross of Jesus Christ (Hebrews 10:1-4)). He became the final sacrifice for all sins because He was perfect; He did not need anyone to die for Him (Hebrews 9:11-14). Everyone who obeys the gospel by confession, repentance, and baptism will be washed clean by the blood He shed on that cross more than 2,000 years ago.

Sin is our greatest problem, so forgiveness is our greatest need. Without forgiveness, we would die in our sins and be condemned for eternity. David understood the length and depth of God's grace: "Bless the Lord, O my soul, and forget none of His benefits; who pardons all your iniquities, who heals all your diseases; who redeems your life from the pit, who crowns you with loving-kindness and compassion; who satisfies your ears with good things, so that your youth is renewed like the eagle" (vs. 2-5).

Jesus makes it clear, however, that if we receive forgiveness, we must also extend forgiveness to others as often as it's required. Part of what we call The Lord's Prayer includes: "And forgive us our debts, as we also have forgiven our debtors" (Matthew 6:12). He later taught the parable of the Unmerciful Servant. It's about a slave who owed his master ten thousand talents, which equaled about

Time Out #3

Choose two students to participate in the "Tissue Race." Each person will try to empty a box of tissues, using only one hand as fast as possible. Whoever can empty their tissue box the fastest wins. Our arms can get tired playing a game like this. Imagine that every tissue represented one of our sins that God has forgiven. We might expect the box to become empty eventually, imagining that there will be a limit to how many sins God will forgive. Yet as long as we're doing our best to live for Him, God continually forgives us.

fifteen years of wages. When the slave begged for mercy, the master forgave the entire debt. The slave was then approached by a fellow slave who owed him just 100 denarii—100 days' wages. The slave begged for mercy, but the first slave refused to forgive the debt and had his fellow slave thrown into prison. When the master became aware of the situation, he had the first slave captured and beaten until he repaid the ten thousand talents. Jesus ends the parable with this shocking statement: "My heavenly Father will also do the same to you, if each of you does not forgive his brother from your heart" (Matthew 18:21-35).

Think of all the times that you've asked God to forgive you. You do so because you wholeheartedly expect Him to forgive you. When someone asks you for forgiveness, how quickly do you forgive him/her? Do you demand that certain conditions be met before you grant forgiveness? Do you act as if you've never sinned? In order to receive the soul-saving blessing of forgiveness, we must freely grant it to others as well.

Sovereignty

It's difficult to express fully how big God is and how powerful God is. David, with his limited human vocabulary, does his best to describe where God is today and what He is doing.

> "The LORD has established His
> throne in the heavens,
> And His sovereignty rules over all.
> Bless the LORD, you His angels,
> Mighty in strength, who perform His word,
> Obeying the voice of His word!
> Bless the LORD, all you His hosts,
> You who serve Him, doing His will.
> Bless the LORD, all you works of His,
> In all places of His dominion;
> Bless the LORD, O my soul!"
> Psalm 103:19-22

The sovereignty of God isn't an easy concept to grasp. The best way to define it is by simply letting Scripture speak for itself. Consider these passages:

"Behold, to the LORD your God belong heaven and the highest heavens, the earth and all that is in it" (Deuteronomy 10:14).

"You, O LORD, rule forever; Your throne is from generation to generation" (Lamentations 5:19).

"For nothing will be impossible with God" (Luke 1:37).

"I am the Alpha and the Omega, the beginning and the end. I will give to the one who thirsts from the spring of the water of life without cost. He who overcomes will inherit these things, and I will be his God and he will be My son." (Revelation 21:6-7).

To say that God is sovereign is to say that nothing is bigger than God, and God isn't limited by anything. Whatever happens in heaven and on earth is known by God and allowed by God. Even though God is sovereign, we still have the ability to choose what we say and do: God doesn't dictate our actions. If He did, there would be no reason for Judgment Day. Why would God judge each person on the last day if He *forced* everyone to behave the way they did in their lives? (2 Cor. 5:10).

David didn't see the sovereignty of God as something to fear. He rejoiced in it! He was thankful that God knew him better than anyone on earth. He rejoiced that God's Word directed his life. If you're a child of God, isn't it a wonderful feeling knowing that the Creator of the universe is on your side? The apostle Paul asked, "What then shall we say to these things? If God is for us, who is against us?" (Romans 8:31).

Steel and Velvet

Carl Sandburg won a Pulitzer Prize for his six-volume biography of Abraham Lincoln. He was asked to give a speech to a joint session of Congress on February 12, 1959, the one hundred fiftieth anniversary of Lincoln's birth. He began his address by saying, "Not often in the story of mankind does a man arrive on earth who is both steel and velvet, who is hard as a rock and soft as a drifting fog, who holds in his heart and mind the paradox of terrible storm and peace unspeakable and perfect."

Abraham Lincoln was just a man. Psalm 103 presents God as the supreme ruler of the universe, One who has demonstrated steel and velvet qualities unmatched by human beings. He has the power to destroy

Time Out #4

Take a few minutes as a class to look closely at something made of steel, as well as a piece of velvet. What do you notice about the contrast? Why is it fitting to think about the "steel" and "velvet" qualities of God?

armies and the gentleness to forgive the sinner. He prepared a place for the devil and his angels called hell, but He also prepared a place of endless rest for those who are faithful called heaven.

We praise God for his sovereignty!

Putting It All Together

1. Jesus answered the lawyer's question by telling the parable of the Good Samaritan. What was Jesus illustrating in that parable?
2. Who are some "neighbors" that are easy for us to ignore or overlook? What are some specific things we can do to show them mercy?
3. Since God has forgiven us, we must forgive others. What often keeps us from forgiving those who have hurt us?
4. In this chapter, we used the term *sovereignty.* When we say that God is sovereign, what does that mean?
5. Why should God's power be a comforting thought to Christians?

Taking It Home

When you get home, think about someone you need to forgive. It might be a friend who said something hurtful to you. It may be someone who sits near you in school and has spread rumors about you. Whoever it is, take the time to pray for them this week. Forgive them, and tell them you have forgiven them. It isn't easy, but the more we pray for others, the easier it is to love and forgive them. When we do that, we model our lives after God.

Chapter 12

The Gospel in Psalms

Psalm 110

Psalm Song Suggestion – "The Gospel Is For All"

Time Out #1

Imagine for a few minutes that you're the president of the United States, and you can choose three different laws you know will get passed. After you decide on your three laws, take a few minutes to share what you decided and why with the rest of the class. What would be the consequences of those laws? How might people react?

Being in charge might sound like fun for a while, but eventually we would all realize our own weaknesses when it comes to making decisions. Psalm 110 reminds us that though we sometimes want to be in charge, Jesus is our ultimate Lord and Savior.

Jesus and Psalm 110

The Pharisees, the men who prided themselves on having a complete, thorough understanding of the Law of Moses, spent nearly three years hounding Jesus with questions. They tried to catch Him giving an answer that would sound blasphemous (disrespectful to God) so they could declare Him to be a false prophet. Near the end of Jesus's ministry, however, Jesus had an opportunity to turn the tables and ask the Pharisees a question.

"What do you think about the Christ, whose son is He?" They said to Him, "The son of David." He said to them, "Then how does David in the Spirit call Him 'Lord,' saying, 'The LORD said to my LORD, sit at my right hand, until I put your enemies beneath Your feet'? If David then calls Him 'Lord,' how is He his son?" No one was able to answer Him a word, nor did anyone dare from that day on to ask him another question" (Matthew 22:42-46).

Jesus quoted Psalm 110. It's a psalm written entirely about the person and ministry of Jesus, although it was written centuries before Jesus was born. These experts in the law knew Psalm 110 well, but they didn't understand a valuable truth that was contained in it: The Messiah was not the son of David; he was the Lord of David. Jesus Christ is not only the Savior; He is the Lord, the Master. Even though Jesus had always answered their loaded questions, the Pharisees could not answer Jesus that day, so they resolved to stop asking Jesus about anything.

Those who challenge the lordship of Jesus will always fail. Those who think they can outsmart Jesus by playing games with Scripture will always fail. Psalm 110 is a key to understanding who Jesus is and why we should stop fighting Him and simply submit to Him.

The Only Lord

It's fascinating how through the inspiration of the Holy Spirit (2 Peter

Time Out #2

Years ago, in his book *Mere Christianity*, C.S. Lewis explored the different opinions people might have about Jesus. If Jesus claimed to be the Son of God, yet knew that wasn't true, then Jesus would be a liar. If Jesus claimed to be the Son of God, believed it to be true, and yet it wasn't, then He would be a lunatic. Yet if Jesus claimed to be the Son of God, and He was telling the truth, then He is the Lord. Write these three options on the board: Liar, Lunatic, and Lord. Many would say today that Jesus is just a "good teacher" but not the Son of God. That cannot be true, since Jesus claimed to be God's Son. If He were a liar or a lunatic, He would not make a good moral teacher. As it turns out, Jesus doesn't leave us the option to call Him a good teacher. He is the Lord and wants to be Lord of our lives.

1:20-21) David refers to Jesus as "my Lord" in verse one. (Notice that God the Father is called "LORD" with capital letters in your Bible, while Jesus is called "Lord" with just one capital letter.) David knew that the Lordship of Christ didn't begin at His birth and end at His death. Jesus is Lord throughout time (Colossians 1:15-17). This fact escapes most of the world today, but Scripture declares that in the end the lordship of Christ will be undeniable. On that day, every tongue will confess that Jesus Christ is Lord (Philippians 2:9-11).

It's easier to convert sinners if you just describe Jesus as the Savior, the One who can wipe away their sins. After all, who doesn't want to be saved from something bad? But when you start teaching that Jesus is Lord, the One who gives commandments and bases your love for Him on whether or not you keep those commandments (John 14:15), the sinners aren't as likely to be converted. "I want to do whatever makes me happy" is a common belief in our culture today. For some, following commandments gets in the way of that happiness.

The lordship of Christ is even troubling for Christians. When Jesus described what life in the kingdom (the church) should look like, He said, "No one can serve two masters; for either he will hate the one and love the other, or he will be devoted to one and despise the other. You cannot serve God and wealth" (Matthew 6:24). Unfortunately, many Christians want to bounce back and forth between the lordship of Christ and the lordship of money, wealth, fame, and ungodliness. They think they can live their lives in both worlds, even though Scripture states that "friendship with the world is hostility toward God" (James 4:4). Living for Jesus requires daily sacrifice, service, and commitment. Jesus cannot just be the Lord of our Sunday mornings; He must be the Lord of our lives.

The King

David knew what it meant to be a king; he ruled Israel for 40 years. He knew that kings and kingdoms could be destroyed. He knew that kings could be manipulated by other kings and form ungodly alliances. But he stated that when Jesus is king, He is undefeated and unmatched: "The LORD says to my Lord: 'Sit at My right hand until I make Your enemies a footstool for Your feet'...Your people will volunteer freely in the day of Your power; in holy array, from the womb of the dawn, Your youth are to You as the dew" (Psalm 110:1, 3).

As of July 2014, there were 45 sovereign rulers on earth. Those men and women are the heads of their respective countries, and they have various titles, such as King, Queen, Prince, Grand Duke, and Emir. All of those men and women fear their enemies; they worry about their legacies; and they dread what could happen to their countries once they're out of power.

Our King has none of those concerns. Read verse one again and picture Jesus resting on a throne, with His enemies propping up His feet. Isn't that the ultimate vision of victory? His enemies cannot win. Christ will have eternal victory over all His challengers.

A king isn't a king unless there are citizens in his kingdom. David wrote that the citizens in Jesus' kingdom will "volunteer freely." Why? Because they will see the power of the Lord. This became reality in Acts 2 when the first gospel sermon was preached. Thousands of people from all over the world assembled in Jerusalem for Pentecost, an annual feast of the Jews. They saw tongues of fire above the heads of the apostles, and they heard a noise like a violent rushing wind. Peter preached that Jesus was Lord and Savior, and that everyone who could hear him put Jesus on the cross. Pierced to the heart, over 3,000 people were baptized that day, and the Lord added them to the church. Tremendous power was shown, and the people freely responded to the message. Since then, millions of people have responded to that same power and that same message.

Jesus always wins. He is the ultimate king. His subjects (Christians) voluntarily submit to His lordship and are saved for eternity. Praise the Lord!

The Priest

The closest definition of a priest in Scripture is in Hebrews 5:1: "For every high priest taken from among men is appointed on behalf of men in things pertaining to God, in order to offer both gifts and sacrifices for sins." The office of the priest is mentioned about 700 times in the Old Testament. The specific qualifications and responsibilities for priests are given in Numbers 18 and other scriptures. Psalm 110 shows how Jesus would be the perfect priest for man because he is from the order of Melchizedek.

We're introduced to Melchizedek way back in Genesis 14. Before Abram's name was changed to Abraham, he led a force of 318 men against Chedorlaomer and other kings who had gone to war against the king of Sodom and his allies. Abram's main motivation was the retrieval of his nephew, Lot, a resident of Sodom, who had been taken captive by Chedorlaomer's army. Abram was successful, and he returned to the valley of Shaveh, where he met the king of Sodom and "the priest of the Most High God," king Melchizedek. The priest-king Melchizedek presented Abram with bread and wine, and said, "Blessed be Abram of God Most High, possessor of heaven and earth; and blessed be God Most High, who has delivered your enemies into your hand" (Genesis 14:19-20).

You might be asking, "What does all of that have to do with Jesus and Psalm 110?" The book of Hebrews gives us the best explanation. (Any time you need to study the difference between the old law and the new law, read

Hebrews.) First, we are given a description of Melchizedek: "Without father, without mother, without genealogy, having neither the beginning of days nor the end of life, but made like the Son of God, he remains a priest perpetually" (Hebrews 7:3). It would be foolish to take that verse literally. If we did, Melchizedek would still be walking the earth! Rather, the Hebrew writer is simply stating that the priest-king didn't become a priest based on his parents, like the other priests of Israel. He became a priest when God appointed him to be one. Jesus is our priest in that way. The Hebrew writer explains it further in the same chapter:

"The former priests, on the one hand, existed in greater numbers because they were prevented by death from continuing, but Jesus, on the other hand, because He continues forever, holds His priesthood permanently...For it was fitting for us to have such a high priest, holy, innocent, undefiled, separated from sinners and exalted above the heavens; who does not need daily, like those high priests, to offer up sacrifices, first for His own sins and then for the sins of the people, because this He did once for all when He offered up Himself." (Hebrews 7:23-25, 27)

In Psalm 110, it was prophesied that Jesus wasn't going to be like a priest in the line of Aaron—sinful and temporary. He was going to be a priest like the order of Melchizedek—appointed by God, perfect, eternal, without a successor, and unchangeable.

Time Out #3

Ask for a volunteer from the class to play the part of a "high priest" for a few minutes. Bring a high priest costume to class, so that the volunteer can wear it and the students can see the significance of everything the high priest wore. God used the priests to minister on behalf of the people and to remind the people of their need for God's forgiveness. When Jesus comes as the perfect High Priest, that specific role is no longer needed.

Righteous Judgment

Judgment Day will be a great relief for some but a great tragedy for others. Paul told the Athenians that God "has fixed a day in which He will judge the world in righteousness through a Man whom He has appointed, having furnished proof to all men by raising Him from the dead" (Acts 17:31). David prophesied that the Lord "will shatter kings in the day of His wrath" (Psalm 110:5).

The wrath of God is also pictured in 2 Thessalonians 1:6-8: "For after all it is only just for God to repay with affliction those who afflict you, and to give relief to you who are afflicted and to us as well when the Lord Jesus will be revealed from heaven with His mighty angels in flaming fire, dealing out retribution to those who do not know God and to those who do not obey the gospel of our Lord Jesus."

Those verses contradict the common beliefs about Jesus in American culture. People cannot comprehend how or why Jesus who would "repay with affliction" or deal out "retribution." It seems too savage and unholy and ungodly.

What those people fail to understand is that Jesus' judgment isn't like man's judgment. Imagine if you had to judge the eternal souls of all seven billion people on earth. Could you do it? Of course not. You haven't even *met* one million people, much less seven billion. Plus, how could you possibly determine the thoughts and intentions of someone else. You can only judge them based on what they say and do. So, you wouldn't be a good judge of mankind. No one on earth would be.

Jesus is the perfect judge. Wouldn't you think that Jesus—the One who gave up heaven to come to earth and die on a cross—would be the most merciful judge we could imagine? And wouldn't Jesus—the One who had to endure the pain of nails being driven into His hands and feet—be the most offended by sin and would be sure that those who opposed the gospel would receive their just punishment?

For the Christian, the wrath of the Lord is nothing to fear. We anxiously

Time Out #4

As Christians, we look forward to spending eternity with God. We're also called by God to share His message with others. Take a few minutes to focus on the life of a missionary. If your congregation supports one, focus on that particular mission work. What kinds of challenges do they face? Pray that they will have courage to continue spreading God's message.

await the coming of Christ because we know that we will finally receive our crown of righteousness (2 Timothy 4:8). We will live forever in heaven. We will never have to endure another pain once our Lord meets us in the air (1 Thessalonians 4:17).

I Will Lift Up His Head

The Old Testament explains the New Testament, and the New Testament explains the Old Testament. Psalm 110 demonstrates that fact better than any other psalm. It's rich in Old Testament history and filled with prophecies of Jesus ... but it only has seven verses.

Jesus is the great king, the eternal priest, and the righteous judge. He alone is worthy of praise. Psalm 110 ends with this: "He will drink from the brook by the wayside; therefore He will lift us His head." Jesus bent over and experienced life in the gutter: He drank with His head down, so to speak. He endured so much for us. But since He was obedient to His heavenly Father, God reached down and lifted up His head. God will do the same for you if you're obedient to His will. "Humble yourselves in the presence of the Lord, and He will exalt you" (James 4:10).

Putting It All Together

1. In Matthew 22, Jesus quotes Psalm 110 when responding to a question from the Pharisees. Can you think of other times people tried to trap Jesus with questions? How did He respond?
2. What does this psalm teach us about Jesus?
3. Have you ever thought about Jesus as the perfect High Priest? How does Jesus fulfill that role in His sacrifice for us?
4. Why is Jesus the perfect judge?
5. Obedience to God's will is important. How do we show obedience in our daily lives?

Taking It Home

We have reminded ourselves how important it is to share God's message. Write down the name of the missionary you discussed in class, and pray for that mission work at least three times this week. Try to be specific, thinking of the challenges missionaries face and resources they might need. If possible, email that missionary and tell him or her about your prayers this week. Missionaries appreciate knowing that others are praying for them!

Chapter 13

Avoiding Amnesia

Psalm 136
Psalm Song Suggestion – "Give Thanks to the Lord"

Amnesia

Picture your wedding day. All your family and friends are together to celebrate; the ceremony is beautiful; and everyone enjoys standing around and talking for hours at the reception. You eat the cake, run through the line of guests, then drive to the airport. That's when things get strange. The person to whom you just promised to spend the rest of your life develops a sudden case of memory loss and has no idea who you are. That's exactly what happened to Amy McNulty. She and her husband, Sean, had tragedy strike on their wedding day, when one of Sean's good friends was in a terrible car accident. When Sean and Amy heard that his friend was in a coma, they didn't want to continue with travel plans. The family convinced them to go, and once they walked in the airport, Sean realized he left his wallet in their car. He went back to get it but never returned.

The police found him three days later at a nearby motel. He had no idea who he was or who she was. He couldn't remember his favorite foods, any family members, or asking Amy to marry him. The stress of the car accident triggered amnesia, and his brain totally disassociated with any memory of his past. For the entire first year of marriage, he had none of his previous memories. What often happens to people struggling with amnesia happened to Sean; his memory came back with time. A year later, a certain picture of his wife brought all of Sean's memories flooding back. He had all his old memories, including memories of a stressful year.

The concept of amnesia is scary, because we hate the thought of forgetting who we are and what has happened in our lives. Our past is important to us; it helps us understand who we are. If we can't remember our past, we

Time-Out #1

Have everyone take a slip of paper and think of a time in Scripture (either Old or New Testament) where God shows His love for His people. Write it down, and then turn it in to the teacher. Write each statement on the board, followed by the phrase "His love endures forever." Put them in chronological order, and then read them out loud. Each student could read his/her contribution and then everyone reads the phrase "His love endures forever" out loud. You, as a class, have created your own psalm. Have someone write it down and make copies for everyone in the class. Distribute the copies at the next class session.

often don't know what to do next. The same thing is true when it comes to faith. The history of God's people helps us understand who we are as Christians today. Even though we live centuries later than the Israelites, knowing about their history can build our faith.

I know, I know. History doesn't always sound exciting. If you have a few minutes of free time during the day, spending it with a history textbook might not be your first choice. But history is important, and one of the ways the Israelites preserved their history was by telling the story of what God had done for them to future generations. Some of the psalms are specifically dedicated to praising God by focusing on what He did for the Israelites through history. Psalm 136 is one example of a narrative psalm that tells the story of God leading His people. As you read the text, you will see the phrase "For His lovingkindness is everlasting" repeated. Some psalms use a refrain like that to drive home a point, and this is one of the most well-known examples. Be sure to focus on the story told between refrains as you read it.

Israelite Amnesia

In Scripture, the Israelites give us one of the clearest examples of spiritual amnesia. During the first fifteen chapters of Exodus, we read about the Israelites being enslaved by the Egyptians, and we also see how God raises up Moses as a leader and delivers them out of slavery. Exodus 15 reveals Moses and his sister, Miriam, leading songs of praise to God for their deliverance. In the next chapter, the Israelites start complaining about not having anything to eat. They actually start reminiscing about what it was like to eat food in

Egypt. They seem to forget that they were slaves, forced to make bricks and construct buildings for Pharaoh. All they can remember is how good it felt to be full (Exodus 16:3).

Throughout the entire Bible, God constantly reminds the Israelites that He had delivered them from slavery. When the Israelites disobey God, lose their freedom to the Midianites, and cry out to God, He reminds them of that deliverance (Judges 6:9). Through the prophets, God would constantly remind the Israelites of that deliverance. That seems strange to us—surely they couldn't forget about something that important, could they? But God knows us, and He knows our temptation to forget.

In the New Testament, when Jesus was speaking to the Jews, He encountered that same kind of spiritual amnesia. In John 8, He tells them that by resisting God's Son, they were following Satan's lead rather than God's plan. In John 8:32, Jesus says that knowing the truth would set them free. Listen to their response in verse 33—"We are Abraham's descendants and have never yet been enslaved to anyone; how is it that You say, 'You will become free'?" Did you catch that? They have never been slaves to anyone? It seems like they have conveniently forgotten about 400 years in Egypt. They would have been well-trained in the laws of Moses, and they would definitely have known about the Egyptian slavery, but it seems like they had a case of spiritual amnesia. They didn't think that the God who delivered them from physical slavery might have a message for them concerning spiritual slavery.

Time-Out #2

In verses 10-16, the psalmist recites how God delivered the Israelites from Egypt. During this time, we read about the ten plagues. Not only were those plagues signs of God's power, they were also proof that God was greater than the gods of Egypt. In fact, in Exodus 12:12, God describes the final plague as judgment against all the gods of Egypt. The Egyptians believed in many different gods, and it's fascinating to think about how the plagues would have affected their view of these false gods. Here are a few of the gods that we know existed in Egypt; take a minute to consider how the plagues would have proved that Israel served the one true God.

Plague #1 – Water into Blood: One of Egypt's gods was Khnuhm, the guardian of the Nile.

Plague #2 – Frogs: Some of them worshipped Hect, who was symbolized by a frog.

Plague #3 – Gnats (from the ground): There was a god named Geb, who was thought to rule the earth.

Plague #4 – Flies: There were many gods symbolized by insects, including Amon-Ra, who had the head of a beetle.

Plague #5 – Livestock: One of the pagan gods in Egypt was Apis, the bull-god.

Plague #6 – Boils: History tells us about Imanhotep, the physician god.

Plague #7 – Hail: One of Egyptian gods was Nui, the sky-goddess.

Plague #8 – Locusts: There were several gods symbolized by locusts.

Plague #9 – Darkness: Horus was known as the sun-god.

Plague #10 – Death of the firstborn: A god named Meskhenet was thought to preside over the birth of children.

Our Amnesia

Even though several years have passed since that day, I remember it clearly. I was in seventh grade, and had tried out for the basketball team. We were waiting on the results to be posted. It seemed like the coach picked the busiest hallway in the entire school building to post the list of names of students who made the cut, so I had to walk in front of a lot of other people to find out my name wasn't on the list. It didn't surprise me (and if you had ever seen me play basketball, it wouldn't surprise you either), but it still disappointed me. I read it in the morning, and it stuck with me all day. It was like I was sleepwalking through all my classes, all I could think about was not making the team. I still had a lot of good friends I had made that year, and there were a lot of fun things I had already gotten to do at school so far, but I wasn't thinking about any of those things.

Disappointment can do that to us sometimes, can't it? It can give us temporary amnesia, blinding us to all our blessings from God. That's what happened to the Israelites when their hunger kept them from remembering

God's deliverance out of Egypt. It's easy for us to see that tendency in the pages of Scripture, but it's harder to spot it in our everyday life. When you've spent a whole week studying for a test and still don't make a good grade, it can ruin the entire day and make you forget about how well you're doing in other classes. Wanting the right clothes might make you forget about all the stuff you already have in your room. One weekend where you don't do anything with your friends can make you forget about how many times you do get to hang out with

Time-Out #3

You've already made a list of the ways God helped biblical individuals in the past; now it's time to make your own list. As a class, brainstorm the ways God has helped you, either individually or as a youth group. Allow yourself a few minutes to come up with as many as you can. You might jot a few down on a piece of paper to save for the "Taking It Home" activity.

them and have fun. We have to combat amnesia the same way the Israelites did; we need to remind ourselves of all the blessings God has given us.

Jogging Our Memory

One way that we can focus on what we have is to think about others who don't have those blessings. A few years ago, I was on a mission trip to Ukraine, and our team spent two weeks living in a Ukrainian orphanage and teaching children Bible stories. The food was different from what we usually eat here, and the orphanage was far enough away from town that we couldn't walk to a grocery store to pick up a snack. There were more than 15 adults staying there and there was only one shower. The days were hot, and after playing with the kids, it was easy to get tired.

One night, when the trip was almost over and I was feeling a little homesick for American food and my own bed, I saw something that changed my life. Each night, the ladies would read to the girls before they went to bed, and the guys would do the same thing for the boys. I had been in the room where the boys stayed before, but I hadn't seen the primitive state of the rest of their area. Their restroom was in terrible shape. I knew they were eating different food than we were, and I snuck in to see it the next day. It was a kind of soupy broth that didn't look nearly as good as our food, and there wasn't nearly as much of it. I looked at the suitcases sitting near my bed, and then I remembered how none of the boys had more than one or two personal things (toys, books, etc.) by their beds. The sadness of their circumstances was overwhelming.

That's when it really dawned on me that the workers at this orphanage were showing us incredible hospitality by giving us the best they had. I was so caught up in thinking about what I had back home that I was missing out on their kindness. I was also blinding myself to how many of these kids struggled through every day with much less than I had, and most of them had a great attitude.

If you stop for a minute, you can probably think of people across the world who do without things we take for granted. You might even know about people you go to school with who don't have what you have. Not only should we be looking for ways to help them, but we should also be reminded of how blessed we are.

Time-Out #4

Think about our usual prayers. What tops the list when we pray to God? Praying for the sick, asking God for things we want, focusing on the problems we face during the day. It isn't bad to pray for all those things, but where does thanksgiving rank on the list? Have you ever heard a prayer that was nothing but thanksgiving to God?

We're tempted to rush past remembering God's blessings and moving straight to our requests. Yet, the Psalms include several songs of thanksgiving. End class with a prayer that consists only of thanksgiving to God. If the class is having trouble coming up with a list, stop and think about what people around us have to do without.

Putting It All Together

1. Imagine what it would be like to experience amnesia. How would you feel? Why is amnesia so scary?
2. God delivered the Israelites from Egypt, a nation that believed in several different pagan gods. What kinds of "gods" does our society focus on today?
3. Were there any biblical examples of God helping His people that were new to you? Can you think of any that were left out of the discussion?
4. As Christians, what are the blessings God gives us that are easy to take for granted?
5. Why do you think it is so easy to focus on our own needs in prayer instead of thanking God for our blessings?

Taking It Home

Find a time this week to reflect on the list you wrote down of things God has done in your life to bless you. Take some time in prayer to thank God for those things. Sometimes, we're general in our prayers, so be sure to thank God for those specific blessings.

Leader's Guide

Teacher Prep for Lesson #1

Introduction – Consult two or three good commentaries to get an overview of identifying the various types of psalms and understanding the poetry of the psalms. You will need to remind the students throughout the study that reading poetry in Scripture is different from reading the history in Genesis or the practical teachings in the New Testament letter.

Time-Out #1 – Encourage all students to write down a challenge they face, and let them know they don't have to sign their names. Make sure you return to this list throughout the study when a psalm deals with one of those issues.

The goal is…to show how these psalms impact the ups and downs of faith.

Time-Out #2 – For the "Marshmallow Challenge," you'll need two bags of marshmallows and two bags of toothpicks. Once you've selected two volunteers (who won't mind a little embarrassment), have them stand on either side of the table. Tell them that they have agreed to the Marshmallow challenge, they have three minutes, and their time starts now. The key to this challenge is not to tell them any rules. Some might think you have to eat as many marshmallows as possible, and others might try to build a marshmallow tower using the toothpicks. If they ask you for directions, just tell them that the clock is ticking. The other students will likely start giving instructions for what they think each one should do. When it's over, debrief by asking the class what the real problem was. Ask the volunteers what it was like to have no idea what they should do. When it comes to worship, we know exactly what's required of us, because God has told us.

The goal is…to remind ourselves of how helpful rules are and how important they are for our worship.

Time-Out #3 – Here are a few examples of Old Testament laws that aren't carried over into the New Covenant to get you started with your list:

The goal is…to teach the differences and distinctions between the Old and New Covenants.

Time-Out #4 – Prepare to help the students see the importance of keeping the proper perspective on worship with each of these statements.

The goal is…to encourage the students to make sure their words reflect a solid perspective on worship.

Teacher Prep for Lesson #2

Recap from Last Time – Share the psalms you read through the week. What did you learn from them?

Introduction – You might want to begin by showing the opening scene of a favorite movie or two. Even if the movie is familiar to you, preview the clip you plan to show to make sure it's appropriate.

Time-Out #1 – Help the students think of some songs that come directly from the psalms (some of these are listed as "Psalm Song Suggestions"). Here is a list to help you get started:
- "O Lord, Our Lord, How Majestic Is Your Name" (Psalm 8)
- "As the Deer" (Psalm 42)
- "Create in Me a Clean Heart" (Psalm 51)
- "I Will Enter His Gates" (Psalm 100)
- "Surround Us Lord" (Psalm 125)

Time-Out #2 – As you think about the words to these songs, you may want to sing one or two. Be prepared to reflect on what these songs mean.

Time-Out #3 – You'll probably want to have a few possible scenarios in mind to help the class as they brainstorm. Try not to spend too much time coming up with the situations but spend more of your time developing strategies to deal with them.

Time-Out #4 – This is the most in-depth "Time-Out" section for this lesson, and you may want to set aside several minutes of class time for it. You can bring copies of this "class psalm" to class next week, and it might even become a song you sing regularly throughout this study.

Teacher Prep for Lesson #3

Recap from Last Time – Share the different ways the students found to honor Jesus during the week. It's vital for us to be constantly searching for ways to point people to Jesus.

Introduction – Ask the class to share some times they felt close to God. Many times, those spiritual "mountaintop" experiences take place in nature. You might want to include some pictures taken at church camp or on a weekend retreat.

Time-Out #1 – Be sure to include some strange, random objects in the box. This will not only make it more fun, but it will also be more difficult for them to remember all the objects. Make sure you have something memorable from the box to give the winner.

*The goal is…*to remind the students that it's easy to forget things quickly. The psalms about creation remind us of God's glory in the world He made.

Time-Out #2 – If it's possible to take a walk outside or to have the entire class sitting outside, that would be a great way for students to find something that reminds them of God. Be prepared for a few unexpected answers, but be sure to keep the discussion on track.

*The goal is…*to remind everyone how we can see God through His creation.

Time-Out #3 – As you discuss each of these passages, make sure to emphasize the link between the name change and a different life.

*The goal is…*to realize the importance of names in the Bible and the importance of our identity as Christians.

Time-Out #4 – Self-esteem issues are challenging for teenagers, which means they might be reluctant to share negative "self-talk" out loud. You might want to have a list of your own prepared before class.

*The goal is…*to remind everyone that all human beings are fearfully and wonderfully made by God.

Teacher Prep for Lesson #4

Recap from Last Time – Discuss which creation psalms they read during the week. Were the psalms familiar? What do they teach about creation? Did they give them a greater appreciation for God's power?

Introduction – You probably have some good stories about storms of your own to share. Visuals of stormy weather might also help set the stage for a discussion of how we face challenging times.

Time-Out #1 – Encourage the students to think about specific difficult times Christians face. Some of them might be reluctant to share a personal story, so you may want to keep the discussion hypothetical. When you think of questions Christians might be afraid to ask, don't shy away from the difficult ones. It's important for them to see that the psalms deal with all these questions and emotions.

The goal is …to understand that it's OK to ask God tough questions, even when we might be afraid to say them out loud.

Time-Out #2 – You might want to do some research on the grief process before leading this discussion. Some individuals in your class may have experienced grief because of loss in their family, so be sensitive to that possibility. In many ways, the psalms help us through the grieving process.

The goal is …to notice the value of the psalms when we're struggling and see evidence they were inspired by God, who knows the way our minds and emotions work.

Time-Out #3 – When you divide the class into groups, make sure that the first group includes students who are familiar with Scripture. This way, the group members who are unfamiliar with the Bible won't feel embarrassed. Help them see the connections between people who suffered in Scripture and people they've known who also persevered through challenges.

The goal is …to realize that God's people have always faced challenges and needed to persevere.

Time-Out #4 – Bring plenty of index cards and pens. Encourage students to write specific reasons for praise, since they will need this for the "Bringing It Home" activity.

The goal is …to realize that even in times of lament, we can praise God for what He has done.

Teacher Prep for Lesson #5

Recap from Last Time – Begin by discussing the praises from last week and the difference they make when we feel bad. The habit of praising God in the midst of difficulties will be valuable throughout their lives.

Introduction – Though the wristwatch is a classic example of the design argument, there are other examples you could use to illustrate the principle. If you're interested in researching further, William Lane Craig's book *On Guard: Defending Your Faith with Reason and Precision* would be a good resource. Chapter 5 of his book deals with the design argument.

Time-Out #1 – The story of Antony Flew is a powerful one to illustrate how understanding God's creation can change someone's view of God. The quote by Flew in the chapter is found in an extended interview conducted by Gary Habermas. Titled "Atheist Becomes Theist—Exclusive Interview with Former Atheist Antony Flew," it was published in the journal *Philosophia Christi* in December of 2004. For more information on Flew's life, you can read *There Is a God: How the World's Most Notorious Atheist Changed His Mind*, by Flew and Roy Abraham Varghese. The entire Warren-Flew Debate can be found online, and you may want to take a visual or excerpt to show in class. It should be emphasized that Flew became a deist, someone who believes in the existence of a Creator, rather than a Christian who sought to follow God. Even so, it's impressive that the natural world caused someone to change such a long-held position.

The goal is...to illustrate the power of God's creation to show evidence of His existence.

Time-Out #2 – Read the collection of scriptures to the class, and see if any students recognize the location of some of these passages. Count how many they could recognize just by hearing the words. Here are the passages that were used: Psalm 119:9-11,34-35,93,105,111,165; John 6:68; John 17:17; Psalm 19:7-8, 10; 2 Timothy 3:16-17; 2 Timothy 4:2; Hebrews 4:12; 1 Peter 2:1-3; 1 Corinthians 1:18; 1 Timothy 4:13; James 1:21; 2 Timothy 2:15; James 1:22-25; Matthew 7:24-27; Mark 13:31; and 1 Peter 1:24-25.

The goal is...to realize what Scripture has to say about the power and authority of the words God inspired.

Time-Out #3 – You'll probably want to purchase the supplies and practice this illustration before class. Use a cup of clear water and food coloring to illustrate what sin does to our lives. Fill a clear cup with water until it's halfway full. Use a dropper to place food coloring in the glass of water. Use several different colors, until the water is dark. As you pour in the food coloring, share some specific examples of sins that can enter our lives. Then pour one cup of bleach into the water, and watch as the stains dissapate and the water becomes clear.

The goal is ...to illustrate the effect sin has on us and the power God's forgiveness has on our sins.

Time-Out #4 – Be prepared with several examples of excuses to help get the conversation started. The way we think about sin is important, so spend time discussing how we should respond when we're tempted to use one of those excuses. Help students discover a godly response for each one.

The goal is ...to train ourselves to think clearly when we encounter temptation.

Teacher Prep for Lesson #6

Recap from Last Time – Review the different ideas the students had about spending more time in the Bible. Be ready to share a few ideas of your own. Encourage them to read five psalms per day, as described in Lesson #5. No matter which plan they choose, the important thing is to find a way to spend more time in Scripture.

Introduction – At some point, all teenagers must deal with feelings of loneliness. That makes psalms like this one especially meaningful. Take advantage of the opportunity to make a connection between this psalm and their daily lives.

Time-Out #1 – Here is a list of several well-known quotes and slogans. Because our culture changes quickly and every community is different, feel free to substitute phrases of your own you feel the students will recognize. If you can think of other verses with which they would be familiar, you can use those as well.

Famous Sayings

- "One small step for man, one *giant leap for mankind.*" (Neil Armstrong)
- "You win some, *you lose some.*" (Common Proverb)
- "15 minutes can save you... *15 percent...*" (Geico Commercial)

Bible Verses

- "In the beginning, God... *created the heavens and the earth...*" (Genesis 1:1)
- "For God so loved the world, that He... *gave His only Son...*" (John 3:16)
- "I can do all things through... *Him who strengthens me...*" (Philippians 4:13)

The goal is... to illustrate how the first line of a psalm can remind us of the entire psalm.

Time-Out #2 – Prepare copies of Psalm 22 for everyone. Here are two parallels between the psalm and the crucifixion of Jesus:

Despised by the People

- Psalm 22:6-8... "But I am a worm and not a man, a reproach of men and despised by the people. All who see me sneer at me; separate with the lip, saying, Commit yourself to the Lord; let him deliver him; let him rescue him, because he delights in him!"
- Matthew 27:42-43... "He saved others; He cannot save Himself. He is the King of Israel; let Him now come down from the cross, and we will believe in Him. He trusts in God; let God rescue Him now, if He delights in Him."

Enduring the Pain

- Psalm 22:14-18 – "I am poured out like water, and all my bones are out of joint; my heart is like wax; it is melted within me. My strength is dried up like a potsherd, and my tongue cleaves to my jaws; and You lay me in the dust of death. For dogs have surrounded me; a band of evildoers has encompassed me; they pierced my hands and my feet. I can count all my bones. They look, they stare at me; they divide my garments among them, and for my clothing they cast lots."

- Matthew 27:35 — "And when they had crucified Him, they divided up His garments among themselves by casting lots.

The goal is…to remind everyone how we can see God through His creation.

Time-Out #3 – This is a great opportunity to highlight some of the older members of your congregation and encourage the students to look for those kinds of examples.

The goal is…to see how God helps Christians endure through difficult times.

Time-Out #4 – You might want to have some smaller pieces of paper already prepared so that the students can post it somewhere in a bedroom or keep it in a wallet.

The goal is…to help students remember to pray when facing temptations.

Teacher Prep for Lesson #7

Recap from Last Time – Begin with a chance for students to share a challenge they faced last week. What difference did it make to remember the passages about Job and Paul?

Introduction – A baby is a great illustration of total dependence. If you have children, this might be a good chance to share some baby pictures to make the point. Better yet, you can dig up some of your own embarrassing baby photos!

Time-Out #1 – This may be a familiar psalm to many in the class, so it might not take long for everyone to memorize it. Taking it phrase-by-phrase will help the class memorize it more quickly.

The goal is...to memorize a portion of God's Word.

Time-Out #2 – Give the background to Joseph's story, and ask the class to think about how it would feel to be in that position.

The goal is...to help consider the challenge of forgiveness.

Time-Out #3 – Be prepared with some suggestions of blessings to share with the groups who are brainstorming.

The goal is...to remind us of how much God has given us.

Time-Out #4 – To help them form their own Psalm 23, go through each of these themes: Count Your Blessings; The Greatest Pleasure is Being with the Lord;. Life Is Easier When the Lord Is Your Guide. Have them write at least two sentences about each one of the themes. Make sure they all have paper so that they can write down their psalm, and follow up with texts throughout the week to remind them to re-read their psalms.

The goal is...to help them reflect on their own relationships with God and put their thoughts into writing.

Teacher Prep for Lesson #8

Recap from Last Time – Review the writings that everyone created. Did reading those during the week change your perspective on God's blessings?

Introduction – Teenagers face a variety of fears, which means that teaching about reliance on God in the face of fear is important. That also means that they may be reluctant to discuss their fears. Be prepared to use your own life as an example to discuss fear. That's a non-threatening way to broach a topic like this one. For the introductory example, you may want to use a visual of President Roosevelt to give the example some historical context.

Time-Out #1 – Here are five relatively common fears in our world today:

1. Arachnophobia — the fear of spiders
2. Aerophobia — the fear of flying
3. Agoraphobia — the fear of inescapable situations
4. Claustrophobia — the fear of confined spaces
5. Brontophobia — the fear of thunderstorms

The goal is…to begin thinking about fears we face and move specifically to fears Christians face.

Time-Out #2 – A little competition between the groups might encourage the students to participate. Here are a few individuals in Scripture who received victory from God over an overwhelming enemy:

1. Joshua 6 — God gives Joshua and the Israelites victory over Jericho.
2. Exodus 14 — Moses and the Israelites cross the Red Sea and Pharaoh's army is defeated.
3. Judges 6 — Gideon and a small army of 300 men defeat Midian.
4. 1 Kings 18 — Elijah faces off with the prophets of Baal.
5. 2 Kings 6 — God blinds the Syrian army, allowing Elisha to lead them away.

The goal is…to remind ourselves that God is greater than any situation we will face.

Time-Out #3 – The traditional cartoon version of the devil is a common image, used in TV shows and team mascots. You might want to include a visual to help the students focus on that concept of Satan. Though we always need to remember that God is far more powerful than Satan, we need to understand that Satan's power and temptations are real.

The goal is . . . to understand the reality of temptations and the importance of preparing ourselves before we encounter them.

Time-Out #4 – Choose someone who likes to draw to write the suggestions on the board, and to draw a picture of a person (stick figures count).

The goal is…to reflect on what we need to do to live like a genuine teacher from God.

Teacher Prep for Lesson #9

Recap from Last Time – As you begin class, see if anyone can quote the first verse of Psalm 27. Ask if anyone thought of that this week when facing a fear. Encourage students to memorize it and repeat it to themselves any time they're afraid.

Introduction – Illustrate the story by Tim Keller. We like to think we have a lot of power, but this psalm reminds us Who is really in control.

Time-Out #1 – Be prepared to help students think through all the changes that take place in a given year, and try to list as many things as possible.
The goal is... to remind us of how many changes we experience in life and how God helps us through those times.

Time-Out #2 – Read the story to the class, and discuss why the children were willing to jump into their father's arms. Explore the idea of why trust in God allows us to be faithful to Him.
The goal is... to remind us that we can and should trust God.

Time-Out #3 – Set a timer or stopwatch to keep track of the two minutes of silence. Don't be surprised if it feels like a long time. Resist the urge to talk before the time is over; let the class feel how long those two minutes last.
The goal is... to illustrate how silence feels to people who live in a busy world.

Time-Out #4 – This exercise should help them think through the psalm. Be prepared to help them with any difficult phrases.
The goal is... to understand the message of the psalm in a modern context.

Teacher Prep for Lesson #10

Recap from Last Time – Give everyone a chance to share what happened during the time they "disconnected" in the past week. What do we notice when we aren't thinking about our computers, phones, or tablets?

Introduction – Familiarize yourself with 2 Samuel 11 and 12 so that you can tell the story of David. You might want to give some students the opportunity to describe their thoughts about David before launching into what happens in those chapters. Even someone who had displayed such great faith understood what it was like to be caught in the darkness of sin.

Time-Out #1 – Be prepared to help students start brainstorming both names of people in the Bible, as well as the sins they committed.
*The goal is…*to help students relate to people in Scripture who had real sins and life issues.

Time-Out #2 – Distribute copies of Psalm 51, and make sure you have one copy for each student. It will be powerful to see how many references to forgiveness are there.
*The goal is…*to feel David's passionate plea for cleansing through this psalm.

Time-Out #3 – Encourage students to be specific as they think through the consequences of each sin listed.
*The goal is…*to help the students think through the results of sin, so that they will take temptation seriously.

Time-Out #4 – Be sure to reserve 2-3 minutes of class for silent prayer. Even a short time of silence may seem uncomfortable, but prepare the class to take advantage of this time.
*The goal is…*to encourage the students to pray actively for their challenges and take responsibility for growing in that area.

Teacher Prep for Lesson #11

Recap from Last Time – Review Psalm 51, and ask the class to think about the areas of their lives they chose to pray about and take responsibility for changing. They don't have to share them with anyone, but all of us need to challenge ourselves and be willing to change as we grow spiritually.

Introduction – The teenage years aren't always filled with friends and classmates showing kindness and love. School can sometimes feel like a battleground, and it's easy to fall into the habit of only looking out for yourself. God's love and forgiveness of us reminds us to reflect those same qualities in our lives.

Time-Out #1 – Allow enough time for the students to think about the question and seriously consider what they would do with the money. Encourage them to think about how much money they would give each family member.

The goal is...to notice our natural desire to show love to those who are close to us and to challenge us to show that same love to everyone.

Time-Out #2 – You might want to bring a visual of a piano keyboard to illustrate this principle. Have the class suggest some temptations that we see often in the 21st century, such as Internet pornography or bullying on social media. Ask them to think about the core of that temptation (for example, lust and anger), and consider how those temptations were present in the first century.

The goal is...to recognize that Jesus was tempted and understands our temptations, even when we think no one else does.

Time-Out #3 – Bring two new boxes of tissues, and challenge each participant to use only one hand to pull out each tissue. They must be pulled out one at a time, and the person who can empty the entire box first wins. The repetitive motion can remind us of how tiring it is to do the same thing over and over, just as we get tired of forgiving others repeatedly. Yet, when God forgives us, there's no limit. The box never empties.

The goal is...to remind the students of the incredible nature of God's forgiveness.

Time-Out #4 – Bring a steel item and a piece of velvet to class. Help students focus on the contrast between the two surfaces. It's a tangible way to understand the holiness and the love of God.

The goal is...to understand that the holiness of God demands a sacrifice for our forgiveness, and the love of God provided that sacrifice—Jesus.

Teacher Prep for Lesson #12

Recap from Last Time – Discuss the forgiveness challenge from last week. Why is it hard for us to forgive others, even when we know we should?

Introduction – We're constantly bombarded with messages about Jesus that reflect the influence of our culture. Psalm 110 paints a vivid picture of Jesus, and it helps us understand the role Jesus plays in our lives. During class, you might want to mention a few of the ways our society has misunderstood Jesus.

Time-Out #1 – Encourage the students to be creative and specific with the laws they create. Share a few as a class, and try to think of unexpected consequences of each one.
*The goal is…*to realize that being in charge is difficult, and none of us would be the perfect lord of all things. Only Jesus fits that description.

Time-Out #2 – Because so many think of Jesus as merely a good moral teacher, these principles by C.S. Lewis will be especially helpful. You may want to put together a visual that spells out the options: Liar, Lunatic, or Lord.
*The goal is…*to understand that Jesus claimed to be the Son of God, and He was telling the truth. It isn't an option for us to think of Him as only a good teacher - He is our Lord.

Time-Out #3 – This one might be tough. If your congregation has used costumes for Vacation Bible School or Children's Bible class programs, you might be able to find a High Priest costume that has already been made. Even if the costume isn't detailed or elaborate, it is helpful to have a visual image of what the High Priests would have looked like in Israel. Exodus 28 provides the background for High Priests and what they wore.
*The goal is…*to gain a greater understanding of the role of the High Priest and to appreciate why the book of Hebrews refers to Jesus as the perfect High Priest.

Time-Out #4 – If your congregation supports mission effort(s), bring names and pictures of the missionaries to share with the class.
*The goal is…*to help your students consider the perspective of a missionary and to feel connected with another ministry of your congregation.

Teacher Prep for Lesson #13

Recap from Last Time – Ask about the missionaries they prayed for last week. See if any of the students were able to email a missionary and correspond with him or her. How does praying for a missionary give us a better perspective on the challenges they face?

Introduction – You may want to do some research on amnesia before class, and you might be able to find a more current example of amnesia to use. The important thing is to emphasize the importance of memory, especially at the spiritual level.

Time-Out #1 – In this exercise, be sure to conclude it by reading the psalm out loud. It will be powerful to hear the repetition of the phrase, "His lovingkindness is everlasting."
The goal is...to to allow the students to have their own "psalm" experience, similar to the Jews who would think about their past as a nation.

Time-Out #2 – You might want to put together some visuals to help illustrate the different gods mentioned (picture of a bull, flies, etc.) If anyone asks how an intelligent nation could believe in such false gods, remind the class about the "idols" that exist and tempt us today, such as sports, entertainment, and wealth.
The goal is...to illustrate that the plagues were displaying God's power over any other so-called "god."

Time-Out #3 – This might be a good opportunity to share a story from your life in which God has helped you. Be sure to leave plenty of time for others to share their stories.
The goal is...to remind ourselves that God does help us when we're in need.

Time-Out #4 – Be prepared with a list of things for which you can be thankful in case discussion is slow. Encourage the students to think beyond the more obvious, common answers and really consider all the ways they've been blessed.
The goal is...to reflect on the blessings God has given us and how important it is that we remember them.